W9-CRR-993

STORIES IN HISTORY

THE
ANCIENT
WORLD

2600 – 100 B.C.

nextext

Cover illustration: Todd Leonardo

Printed in the United States of America

ISBN 0-618-14213-4

5 6 7 8 9 — DCI — 06 05 04 03 02

Table of Contents

PART I: ANCIENT AFRICA

This story takes place during the days when Djoser was pharaoh in Egypt. Chief Minister Imhotep's plan for a new temple seems impossible!

A tomb builder in Thebes tells of a most remarkable princess. She gets herself crowned as the pharaoh. She expands trade on Africa's coast. People talk about her rule of peace for hundreds of years.

PART III: ANCIENT INDIA AND CHINA

c. 140 B.C.

by Marianne McComb

Imagine finding the perfectly preserved body of a Han princess dead nearly 2,200 years! That's exactly what happened to workers digging for a new hospital.

About this Book

The stories are historical fiction. They are based on historical fact, but some of the characters and events may be fictional. In the Sources section you'll learn which is which and where the information came from.

The illustrations are all historic. If they are from a time different from the story, the caption tells you. Original documents help you understand the time period.

Items explained in People and Terms to Know are repeated in the Glossary. Look there if you come across a name or term you don't know.

Historians do not always agree on the exact dates of events in the ancient past. The letter c before a date, means "about" (from the Latin word circa*).*

If you would like to read more about these exciting times, you will find recommendations in Reading on Your Own.

Background

The god Ashur and the great gods who have
    enlarged my kingdom
Have given me strength and power.
They have ordered me to extend the lands
    of their country.
They put powerful weapons into my hand
And made me a cyclone of battle.
I conquered lands and mountains,
Cities and rulers, all enemies of Ashur.
I fought with sixty kings,
Spreading terror among them,
Winning a glorious victory over them.
I added more land to Assyria,
I added more people to its people.

—Tiglathpileser I
King of Assyria

An Assyrian king returns home after
winning a battle (c. 700 B.C.).

Civilization Began in River Valleys

Before Civilization

The earliest people lived in small family groups. They followed herds of animals and collected wild plants to get food. We call people who live this way "hunter-gatherers." Over thousands of years, people discovered they could get food for themselves by planting seeds. When this happened, they no longer moved with the animals. They stayed in one place to care for their crops. They raised goats, sheep, and other animals for food. They made clothing from the wool or skins of their animals. They learned to build homes from materials nearby.

People noticed that the yearly floods of rivers made land very fertile. Then they chose to live near the rivers.

When many people lived near each other, they discovered they needed rules to keep them from taking each other's crops or animals. They needed war leaders to help them fight others who wanted to take over their good land. They needed religious leaders to help them keep the gods on their side.

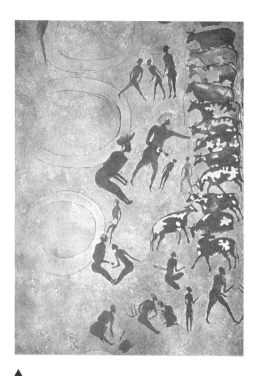

▲

Women and children herd cattle outside circles that stand for their huts in this ancient North African rock art.

People learned to control the floodwaters of their rivers. They brought water in during the dry season and drained it away during the floods. Farmlands became larger, and much food could be grown.

Once there was enough food, everyone did not need to work at farming. Some could build ships to get fish or to travel down the river. Others could build storehouses for the extra grain. These changes led to the building of cities.

Civilization Means Cities

The earliest civilizations in the world developed from river valley cities. These were not villages or towns. They were complex communities. Hundreds to thousands of people lived in them.

There were huge temples, palaces, and buildings for storing grain. There were docks where boats were built. Ships unloaded fish from the seas and goods from countries far away. Houses lined streets, and plumbing took wastewater away from the houses.

Roads joined neighboring cities. Bridges spanned smaller rivers. Walls protected the cities from enemies. In China, walls protected the borders of the empire.

The armies of these people clashed. Weaker cities were conquered and sent taxes to the victors. Sometimes their people were made slaves. With more money, goods, and workers, the cities grew into huge empires.

Leaders arose who had good ideas. They knew what to do to get power and keep it. They set up systems for keeping the peace and for organizing for war. They organized the tasks of workers on huge building projects. They inspired people to follow them. But also they used force and terror to get and keep control.

Laws controlled the lands, the wealth, and the people. People developed writing systems. Then they could record the amount of grain in storage. They could keep track of how much the conquered cities owed. They could write about their kings.

Religious leaders wrote hymns of praise, taught the right way to live, and helped their people understand the meaning of life.

Literature let people share their understandings of the gods, the stories of their heroes, and the love poetry of the young people. Today we can experience the lives of people from more than four thousand years ago because they created literature.

▲

Archaeologists excavate the two-thousand-year-old city of Caesarea in Israel.

Ships like these *feluccas* have sailed the Nile River for thousands of years.

Ancient Africa

The water flows north,
The wind blows south,
And each man goes to his hour.

—Ancient Egyptian poem

The civilizations of ancient Africa may be the earliest in world history. They grew up in the Nile Valley. It is in the northeast corner of the continent where Egypt is today. Here, the Nile flows into the Mediterranean Sea. It makes a water highway for ships. The river flows from the southern mountains down to the Mediterranean and makes traveling north very easy. The winds blow from the north to the south. So with a sailing boat, travel is easy both down the river and on the way back.

Egypt was the "black land and red land." The "black land" was the rich soil of the Nile Valley, renewed each year when the Nile flooded and covered the fields with a layer of fertile mud, or silt. The "red land" was the desert east and west of the Nile that protected Egypt against invasion.

With plentiful food and long periods of peace, Egypt developed a great civilization. Its most famous monuments are the Great Pyramids built at Giza around 2500 B.C. as tombs for the pharaohs. Pharaoh (FAIR•oh), meaning "great house," was the title of the kings of Egypt.

South of Egypt, on the eastern coast of Africa along the coast of the Red Sea, lay the kingdoms of Kush, Meroë, and Aksum. Today, these areas are Ethiopia and northern Sudan. A trip up the Red Sea took people from Africa to the regions in Arabia that are now Israel and Jordan.

When people travel, they meet people with other ways of living. They get new ideas about how to solve problems. The exchange of ideas and goods among the peoples of Africa and their neighbors in the Fertile Crescent helped both civilizations develop.

◀ This statuette of a man was made in ancient Sumeria around 2600 B.C.

The Fertile Crescent

In Uruk, Gilgamesh built great walls and the temple of the goddess Ishtar. Look at its outer wall that shines like copper and its inner wall that has no equal! Touch the threshold, it dates from ancient times! . . . Climb up on the wall of Uruk and walk around. . . . Is it not kiln-fired brick and well-made? Did not the Seven Sages lay its foundations?

—The Epic of Gilgamesh

Rich farmlands along the southeastern coast of the Mediterranean Sea border the scorching Arabian Desert. Through them runs the Jordan River. To the east, beyond the desert, the river valleys of the Tigris and the Euphrates also provide good growing soil. The land between these two rivers is known as Mesopotamia. The entire region is called the Fertile Crescent.

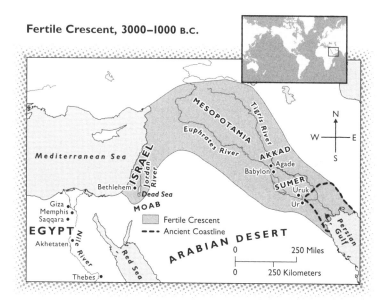

Fertile Crescent, 3000–1000 B.C.

Fertile Crescent

- - - Ancient Coastline

0   250 Miles

0   250 Kilometers

Mediterranean Sea

MESOPOTAMIA

Euphrates River

Tigris River

AKKAD

Agade

Babylon

SUMER

Uruk

Ur

ISRAEL

Jordan River

Bethlehem

Dead Sea

MOAB

Giza

Memphis

Saqqara

EGYPT

Akhetaten

Nile River

Red Sea

Thebes

ARABIAN DESERT

Persian Gulf

N
W — E
S

Here developed the civilizations of two
groups of people: the Semites and the Sumerians.
The Semitic people were desert people who
invaded Mesopotamia. They include the Jews of
the Bible. Tradition says the descendants of
Noah's son Seth were the ancestors of the people
of northern Mesopotamia. The Sumerians lived
in the southern part of Mesopotamia along
the Euphrates.

In Mesopotamia, some cities grew to become city-states. A city-state is like a kingdom, but it has only one large city in it. One of the early city-states was Akkad, which was north of Sumer.

This copper bison was made in Sumer around 2300 B.C. ▶

Other city civilizations developed into empires. An empire includes not only other cities but also conquered peoples whose ways of life are often different. Within an empire, the conquered people keep many of their own ways and their own leaders. They must pay taxes to the empire. They must join in the wars of the empire. They must obey the laws of the empire and the commands of its ruler. In southern Mesopotamia, Sumer included the city-states of Uruk and Ur. Later, the Babylonian Empire developed from the city of Babylon.

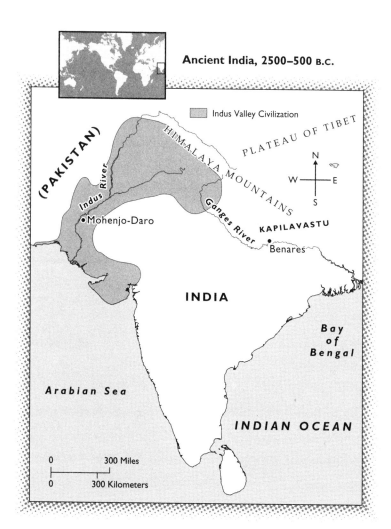

Ancient India, 2500–500 B.C.

Indus Valley Civilization

PLATEAU OF TIBET

HIMALAYA MOUNTAINS

(PAKISTAN)

Indus River

Mohenjo-Daro

Ganges River

KAPILAVASTU

Benares

INDIA

Bay of Bengal

Arabian Sea

INDIAN OCEAN

N
W   E
S

0   300 Miles
0   300 Kilometers

Ancient India

Indus Civilization

Ancient India had a lost civilization. From around 2500 to 1500 B.C., people built large cities in the valley of the Indus River. This area is in northwestern India and present-day Pakistan. The people created a system of writing and traded with other ancient peoples. Around 1500 B.C., the Indus civilization disappeared because of invasions from the north and other causes. The Indus people were completely forgotten until their cities, at sites such as Mohenjo-Daro, were discovered by archaeologists in the twentieth century.

The Caste System

The invaders who destroyed the Indus civilization occupied much of India. Priests and warriors were the most important people among these invaders. The society they built was organized into four large divisions, called castes:

Brahmins (priests)
Kshatriyas (rulers and warriors)
Vaishyas (merchants and farmers)
Shudras (laborers)

Hinduism and Buddhism

The religion of the invaders blended with that of the people they conquered to form Hinduism. The religious beliefs of Hinduism developed slowly over a long period. Hinduism was not founded by one person at one time. By contrast, Buddhism can be traced to a single person and a specific time and place. Siddhartha Guatama, the founder of Buddhism, was a prince from Kapilavastu, a small kingdom in northeastern India. He was born in 563 B.C. He preached that desire was the cause of suffering and that people must end desire to gain salvation. He was called the Buddha, "the enlightened one," by his followers.

Ancient China

The Zhou Empire

Civilization in China began in two river valleys, the Huang He (hwahng•HUH), or Yellow River, in northern China, and the Yangtze (yang•SEE) in central China. By 1400 B.C. the Chinese had developed a highly advanced system of writing with a vocabulary of more than 3,000 characters. Around

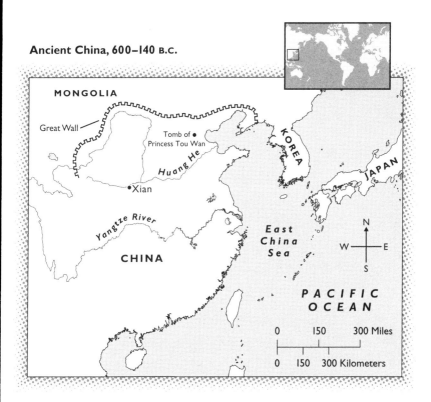

Ancient China, 600–140 B.C.

1027 B.C., the Zhou (joh), a people from Central Asia, conquered China. For the first 300 years, the Zhou empire was generally peaceful. Later, local rulers challenged Zhou rule, and the violent "period of the warring states" followed.

Confucianism and Daoism

Two Chinese philosophers offered very different answers to the problems of Chinese society during this time. Confucius (kuhn•FYOO•shuhs) (551–479 B.C.)

▲

These life-size clay warriors were buried in the tomb of
Chinese Emperor Shi Huangdi (reigned c. 221–207 B.C.).

taught that moderation, kindness, and respect for tradition were necessary for a good society. By contrast, Laozi (LOW•DZUH) (6th century B.C.) taught simplicity, acceptance, and harmony with the *Dao* (dow) or "way." *Dao* was a mysterious power behind all things in the universe.

Shi Huangdi and the Han

Around 221 B.C., China was unified by Shi Huangdi (shihr hwahng•dee), which means "first emperor." He was an energetic ruler who had a vision for China. But he was brutal. He had the Great Wall of China built to protect northern China from invasion. He began with the defensive walls that already existed. He had workers join them into a 1,500 mile-long barrier. Historians believe the building task may have cost a million lives. Shi Huangdi was succeeded by the Han emperors, who ruled China for the next 400 years. Under Han rule, China grew as large and wealthy as the Roman Empire of the same period.

Time Line

c. 2620 b.c.—Imhotep built a step pyramid for the pharaoh, Djoser.

c. 2600 b.c.—40,000 people lived in the city of Mohenjo-Daro in India.

2550–2470 b.c.—Great Pyramids of Giza were built.

2335–2279 b.c.—Sargon ruled in Sumer.

1792–1750 b.c.—Hammurabi ruled in Babylonia and gave a code of laws.

c. 1472–1458 b.c.—Hatshepsut ruled in Egypt.

1390–1353 b.c.—Amenhotep III ruled in Egypt.

1353–1336 b.c.—Akhenaten ruled in Egypt.

970–930 b.c.—Solomon ruled as king of the Israelites.

c. 600 b.c.—Parts of the Great Wall of China are begun.

563–483 b.c.—Siddhartha Gautama, the Buddha, lived in India.

551–479 b.c.—Confucius lived in China.

221–207 b.c.—Emperor Shi Huangdi ruled in China.

c. 300 b.c.—Aksum rose as a civilization in Ethiopia.

c. 140 b.c.—Han Princess Tou Wan died.

Ancient Africa

chapter 3

Imhotep and the First Pyramid

BY LYNNETTE BRENT

"Miralai," a voice said. "The chief minister asks you to come to his chamber."

I looked up, startled to see Dalaja, the chief minister's assistant, standing in front of me. I had been deep in the writing of the plans for the tomb of Pharaoh **Djoser** at Saqqara (suh•KAHR•uh). Dalaja, my father's friend, had helped me to get my job with Chief Minister **Imhotep**.

"I am so sorry, Dalaja. I did not hear you arrive. I will go to Imhotep right away." I gathered my

---

People and Terms to Know

Djoser (ZHOH•suhr)—Egyptian pharaoh who ruled from about 2650 to 2575 B.C. **Pharaoh** (FAIR•oh) was the title of the kings of ancient Egypt. Djoser is best known for building the pyramid at Saqqara. See the map on page 16.

Imhotep (ihm•HOH•tehp)—poet, architect, and physician who served under four Egyptian pharaohs. He was chief architect for Djoser's pyramid at Saqqara. After his death, Egyptians made Imhotep a god.

This statue of Imhotep was carved around 1350 B.C., many centuries after his death.

supplies—**papyrus**, ink, and reed pen—and headed toward the pharaoh's palace.

Dalaja and I hurried through the neighborhood near the palace. Though it was early in the day, we could hear shouts from the marketplace. Crowds of people there were buying and selling food and costly goods, such as perfumed oils and silver jewelry.

I glanced down the street. Down at the river, many people were washing their clothes.

"How can you question Imhotep? His work for the pharaoh has been brilliant."

My work was on my mind. "Dalaja, may I ask a question? I know that Imhotep and Pharaoh Djoser have big plans for the temple at Saqqara. But I am concerned about the design." I chose my words carefully. I didn't want to show disrespect for the pharaoh or his chief minister.

Dalaja looked at me quietly. "Miralai, remember that you are a **scribe**. Do you doubt the pharaoh? How can you question Imhotep? His work for the pharaoh has been brilliant."

People and Terms to Know

papyrus (puh•PY•ruhs)—paper made from the pulp of the papyrus plant, a type of tall grass that grows in water.

scribe—in ancient societies, one of the few people who could read and write. A scribe was an official who wrote the public records.

"I'm sorry, Dalaja. I feel great respect for Pharaoh Djoser," I answered. "He ended years of **famine** in Egypt by rebuilding the temple of the god Khnum. He and Chief Minister Imhotep love Egypt completely. Everyone admires Imhotep. But their plans for this temple seem impossible to me. The more time I spend writing them, the more unbelievable they appear!"

Now Dalaja stopped in his tracks. He placed his hands on my shoulders in a fatherly way. He smiled as if he knew a secret.

"Miralai, do not worry. Imhotep is a magician as much as he is a leader. I don't understand his magic, but I know it exists. Remember, we have never seen the sun god Re, yet we still believe he exists. The sun rises every day as Re promises. Have faith, Miralai. Be glad that you can work with one who is so talented."

Dalaja was right, of course. I felt ashamed. Who was I to question Pharaoh Djoser and Chief Minister Imhotep?

People and Terms to Know

famine—severe, wide-reaching food shortage.

As we came to the palace, I thought about Imhotep's amazing rise to the post of chief minister. Imhotep was not a nobleman. He was one of the common people, like the many I passed in the market every day. Yet his love for Egypt and his spiritual teachings earned him a meeting with the pharaoh. Common people were never allowed to meet the pharaoh. Yet it happened!

Pharaoh Djoser and Imhotep met privately, so only they know what really happened. But word spread that Imhotep had cured the pharaoh of a terrible pain in his mouth. Whatever happened, Imhotep earned Pharaoh Djoser's trust. Soon he became the pharaoh's high priest.

Dalaja and I arrived at the chief minister's room in the palace. Dalaja announced my arrival. Imhotep turned to greet us. He was ready to continue discussing the design of Pharaoh Djoser's temple. I quickly set out my writing tools on a table near the window. Then I set out my notes from our earlier meetings.

Imhotep looked at them carefully. This design, though unfinished, was remarkable. Pharaoh Djoser and Imhotep wanted to create a monument to the pharaoh's reign. They wanted this temple to outlast all of us—and the many generations to come! The pharaoh and his family would be buried in a temple like no other.

Pharaoh Djoser knew exactly what ideas the temple should express. This funeral temple should give honor to the pharaoh and his family. But it also should tell of the rich history of Egypt. In addition, the pharaoh insisted that this temple should honor our religion. Our faith was not given enough importance in the temples of past pharaohs.

The pharaoh and his family would be buried in a temple like no other.

Imhotep had begun designing this temple months ago. He had visited many other temples. He had studied our ancestors in order to honor Egypt's past. Many days I went with him, only to return to my room without writing a word. On other days, I would arrive at the palace to find that Imhotep had been up all night. He had written his ideas himself. He was afraid that he would forget them if he waited for me.

At last, Imhotep developed his plan. The earlier temples built to honor our pharaohs had been flat, rectangular buildings called mastabas. They were made of mud-brick. Most all of our buildings were built this way. Imhotep had a different idea. He would pile one mastaba on top of another. The new design was a **step pyramid**. The temple would have six different levels, each one a step up from the one below. This rising height of the temple would remind us of Djoser's climbing to the sky after his death. No building had been designed like this before.

The pyramid's spiritual nature was continued inside. The building would house a collection of statues, chapels, and temples. All of these honored our people's strong religious beliefs. Outside, there were to be speakers' platforms and gathering areas. The pharaoh would hold religious ceremonies there.

The temple would copy some designs found on the royal palace in Memphis. This would honor Egypt's rich history and culture. There would be forty columns on the walls outside the pyramid to honor the temples of past pharaohs. What a remarkable monument! It looks both to the past and the future!

People and Terms to Know

step pyramid—high, step-shaped building that is both a tomb and a temple.

▲

The Step Pyramid of Pharaoh Djoser was built by Imhotep
around 2620 B.C. It was the first tomb in ancient Egypt to be
built entirely of stone and is the world's oldest pyramid.

Today, Imhotep said, we would discuss building
materials. I was relieved finally to get to this subject.
How would a building made of mud and wood
hold up the weight of six levels? I tried to remember
Dalaja's words. I had to have faith in Imhotep the
magician as well as in Imhotep the chief minister.

Imhotep described his vision of the completed temple. I had to catch my breath! I was wrong to worry about mud and wood. The temple would be built from huge blocks of stone! What an incredible idea! Moving these stones would require the strength of hundreds, even thousands of men. No tool that I know of could lift these huge stones up six levels.

"Is this the magic of Imhotep I have heard so much about?" I asked, barely whispering. Time would certainly tell.

QUESTIONS TO CONSIDER

1. How had Pharaoh Djoser ended the famine in Egypt?

2. How did Imhotep gain the favor of Djoser?

3. How was Imhotep's design like and unlike the Egyptian temples of the past?

4. In what ways was Imhotep a great leader?

5. What does this story tell you about daily life in Egypt during this period?

His Majesty, Herself: Hatshepsut of Egypt

BY DEE MASTERS

I, **Ineni**, have lived long because of my attention to duty. I have honored Amon-Re (A H • muhn • RAY), the god of my city, Thebes. I have seen pharaohs born and pass on from this land, in all their might and pride. I have built for the great **Amenhotep I** and for his son, grandson, and great-grandson. I have built for his majesty herself, **Hatshepsut**, daughter of our god Amon-Re. May their beauty last forever. Lord Amon, grant long life to Egypt's kings.

People and Terms to Know

Ineni (in•NEHN•nee)—Egyptian architect who built for several pharaohs.

Amenhotep I (AH•muhn•HOH•tehp)—Hatshepsut's grandfather, a pharaoh who ruled from about 1514 to 1493 B.C. He invaded Nubia and fought wars with the Libyans and Syrians.

Hatshepsut (hat•SHEP•soot)—first woman to be king (pharaoh) of Egypt. She ruled from about 1472 to 1458 B.C.

Hatshepsut is shown as a man, wearing the ceremonial false beard of a pharaoh.

I, like my lord **Thutmose I**, whose tomb I built, must soon go forth to heaven and join the sun. But I will leave a story on my tomb walls—a story of the greatness of **the black land and the red land**. I would also, in some manner, like to be remembered. As I hope to have my story told, I tell this story.

In my youth, I built for the great warrior Pharaoh Amenhotep, living forever. But hear, men and women, all! I speak the story of Amenhotep's son, Thutmose, and Thutmose's daughter, Hatshepsut. She stood out as the sun among stars, beloved of her father, more beautiful than anything. As he was god on earth, Thutmose knew that Hatshepsut would be the chosen one. As he was the ruler of his people, Thutmose knew his people. He planned well for his daughter.

She hunted in boys clothes. She speared the Nile fish. She threw her hunting stick and brought down the ducks. Her trained cats brought them back to her. She pleased her father with her boyish

---

People and Terms to Know

Thutmose I (thoot•MOH•suh)—Hatshepsut's father, pharaoh of Egypt from about 1493 to about 1482 B.C. He is known for conquering Nubia in Africa and areas in Asia all the way to the Euphrates River.

the black land and the red land—rich, black farmland around the Nile River and the red desert sands.

games. From her mother, she learned what a woman should know: manners, how to behave at court, how to walk with grace and dignity. She learned her prayers, especially those to Amon-Re, her father in the heavens.

Then the days of her childhood ended. Her older sister died. Shortly followed the death of her two little brothers. She was the last royal heir of Thutmose. When his beloved wife died, Thutmose went against everything that had been done before in his kingdom. He placed Hatshepsut on the throne with him. She was nineteen and still wore men's clothes. She wore them all her life. Her father wrote of "the majesty of him, my daughter." He took her all over Egypt to be recognized as the crown prince. Her father did all he could to make her a success. Thutmose left this life at age seventy-five, after ruling thirty-five years. He went forth to heaven to be with the gods. He had worked with gods and men for her. He had chosen her husband for her.

She was nineteen and still wore men's clothes. She wore them all her life.

For a while, she remained the first woman to rule Egypt, not as pharaoh, but as

regent. The time had not yet arrived. But she was **Maat**, the law. And the law said she must marry. So she did what was usually done when there was no son to be king. To protect the purity of her divine family, she married one of her half brothers. Because of the marriage, he became the pharaoh of Egypt, Thutmose II. Hatshepsut became the Great Wife, ruling with him. The time was not yet ripe. They had two daughters, but no sons. Thutmose II did not rule long. Before he went to join the gods, he named his son by a lesser wife to take his place.

At the age of nine, this son, Thutmose III, was married to the little daughter of Hatshepsut. Both children were too young to rule, so Hatshepsut still ruled as the regent. As the records say, "The divine woman Hatshepsut took care of the business of Egypt the way she wished. Egypt did what she asked, because she had come from the gods. She was the cable which held the north of Egypt, the stake to which was tied the south."

People and Terms to Know

regent—temporary ruler until the real ruler can take over.
Maat (muh•AHT)—Egyptian goddess of law and truth.

For two years after her husband's death, she helped the new Thutmose as he entered the Great Temple for special training. For two years, she bowed her proud head to him. She stood behind him. She put her little daughter above herself. She planned. She spoke with others in power. She made promises. Then she did what no other woman had ever done in Egypt. She made herself the king.

She wore the king's short robe with the lion's tail hanging in back. She carried the royal flail and shepherd's crook. She wore the king's false beard, symbol of his manly powers, on her chin. She proclaimed herself pharaoh of Egypt.

Pharaohs were men! How could she do this?

She said there was a miracle! She had been praying in the temple before the great statue of Amon-Re when it spoke to her. "Go, my daughter, king of Egypt!" it said. Now she was not a woman. She was the king, King Hatshepsut I of Egypt. The young king, Thutmose, and his mother watched helplessly as Hatshepsut placed the double crown of the **two Egypts** on her head. She was the first woman to wear that crown.

People and Terms to Know

two Egypts—Upper and Lower Egypt. Upper Egypt was the southern region, up the Nile River. Lower Egypt was the northern region, downstream.

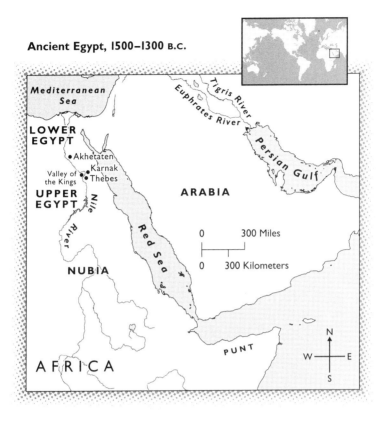

Ancient Egypt, 1500–1300 B.C.

Mediterranean Sea

LOWER EGYPT

• Akhetaten

Valley of the Kings

• Karnak • Thebes

UPPER EGYPT

Nile River

NUBIA

Red Sea

ARABIA

Tigris River

Euphrates River

Persian Gulf

0   300 Miles

0   300 Kilometers

PUNT

AFRICA

N
W — E
S

The king has ruled for fifteen years. Why do I, Ineni the builder, put her story in my tomb? Because, like me, she is a builder. She has not sent out armies of conquest. She has given the people a rule of peace. She has enlarged our trade. She has sent ships to trade through the Red Sea with the land of **Punt** as they did in the old days. These ships brought back gold, rare woods, beautiful

People and Terms to Know

Punt—ancient country in eastern Africa, near present-day Somalia.

trees, strange animals and animal skins, and rich perfumes. She has restored that which was destroyed. She has raised up that which war had torn down. Go and see! See her great monument in the **Valley of the Kings**. It is carved out of the solid red rock. See the two needlelike shafts—each carved from a single stone, each over one hundred feet tall—that she raised at Thebes. What she has built will speak for her forever, and I have built for her.

◀ Egyptian statue of a cat carved during the period of the New Kingdom (1570–1075 B.C.). Hatshepsut hunted with trained cats.

People and Terms to Know

Valley of the Kings—place on the opposite bank of the Nile from Thebes. Hatshepsut's memorial temple and many royal tombs were built there.

I will go to the gods before her story ends, but I wish to be remembered. I fed the hungry, sheltered the widowed, aided the orphaned. I built. I tell this story that I may in turn be remembered. Amon-Re, you are the greatest of gods, the maker of all things that are, maker of what has been. May I be remembered for the beauty I created.

* * *

After Hatshepsut died, Thutmose III came to power again. His conquests brought an area north to Syria and south to Nubia under Egyptian rule. Under Thutmose III, the Egyptian empire reached its greatest size.

QUESTIONS TO CONSIDER

1. In what ways might Hatshepsut's upbringing have helped her later, when she became pharaoh?

2. Why did Hatshepsut mainly wear men's clothing?

3. Why was Hatshepsut made regent?

4. What "miracle" helped Hatshepsut become pharaoh?

5. How did Hatshepsut prove herself a good ruler?

A Place in the Sun
by Jill Rubalcaba

Jill Rubalcaba's fast-paced novel is set in ancient Egypt. Sekhmet, the gifted young son of a sculptor, is condemned to slavery in the gold mines of Nubia when he attempts to save his father's life.

Hatshepsut and Ancient Egypt
by Miriam Greenblatt

Miriam Greenblatt presents the reign of Hatshepsut and examines life in ancient Egypt during her time.

Pharaoh's Daughter
by Julius Lester

Julius Lester gives a vivid picture of ancient Egypt as he retells the biblical story of Moses, who is rescued by an Egyptian princess and becomes a prophet of his people.

Akhenaten and Nefertiti

BY JUDITH LLOYD YERO

Dawn! The chariot of the great god **Aten** appears on the eastern horizon. The city of Thebes stirs. Smoke from the evening fires hangs in the air. The people of the city slowly awake from their night's rest on the rooftops of their mud-brick homes. The fresh breezes they had sought the night before now chill the air. The people come down ladders into the courtyard and prepare their morning meals.

As the sun grows from a sliver of light to the great disk of life, the sounds of the city grow louder. On the shore of the mighty river, men shout and joke. They are loading ships and barges with trade

People and Terms to Know

Aten (AHT•n)—Egyptian god representing the power behind the sun god, Re. Aten is shown as a circle representing the golden disk of the sun.

Nefertiti and Akhenaten are shown holding hands in this small painted statue. Notice their realistic faces and bodies. The Amarna art style of their reign was less formal than that of earlier pharaohs.

goods for distant lands. Donkeys bray, complaining at the loads they carry. The narrow streets in the workers' quarter buzz with activity.

People hurrying about their daily business hardly notice the priests in their fine robes moving toward the temples. Ordinary people are not allowed within the temples. They are the houses of gods. Egyptians have worshiped these gods since before the pyramids were built, more than a thousand years earlier.

◀ This famous portrait of Nefertiti suggests why she is widely considered the most beautiful woman of the ancient world.

Among the gods in the temple, there is Horus, the falcon-headed god. Isis, the mother of Horus, is crowned with the head of a vulture and the disk of the sun. Hathor, the horned-cow goddess of love is there, too. Most important is the creator of all, Amon. The great temple at **Karnak** honors Amon in the rows of ram-headed **sphinxes** guarding the kings of Egypt.

Each day, the priests wash and dress the statue of the god of their temple. But, these days, few people care. Their king and pharaoh, **Akhenaten**, has declared these gods false. Now it is said that the old gods were only humans or animals that became gods over the years. They had human weaknesses and could become angry or spiteful. Their power was often used to punish or strike fear into people's hearts. Now these older gods are seen only as statues.

People and Terms to Know

Karnak (KAHR•nak)—largest religious complex ever built. Karnak was built over thousands of years by many different pharaohs. See the map on page 41.

sphinxes (SFIHNGKS•ez)—figures in Egyptian mythology with the body of a lion and the head of a man, ram, or hawk.

Akhenaten (AH•kuh•NAHT•n)—Egyptian pharaoh who reigned from about 1353 to 1336 B.C.

But Akhenaten said that Aten is different. Aten is the one true god—visible to all who look to the heavens. He blesses the earth by bringing life to the land and the people. He is seen in the flowers and trees. He is in the grains and fruits that provide nourishment to the people. He is in the joy of children at play. Akhenaten even changed his name from Amenhotep, meaning "Amon is content," to Akhenaten, meaning "he who works for Aten."

Aten is different. Aten is the one true god—visible to all who look to the heavens.

Once, the priests spoke with the gods about the people's needs. Now only the pharaoh has that right. He speaks to only one god—Aten—the great power behind the golden disk of the sun.

The priests, their power fading, are angry. They mutter against Pharaoh Akhenaten. Like his father, **Amenhotep III**, Akhenaten has married a woman born in another land—**Nefertiti**. She is a strong

---

People and Terms to Know

Amenhotep III (AH•muhn•HOH•tehp)—Egyptian pharaoh who ruled from 1390 to 1353 B.C. He built many statues and temples, especially at Karnak. He broke tradition by marrying Tiye, a commoner from the African kingdom of Nubia.

Nefertiti (NEHF•uhr•TEE•tee)—queen of Egypt, considered a major advisor to Akhenaten, her husband. Her name means "the beautiful one has come."

queen. The priests say that she has filled the pharaoh's head with strange ideas of **monotheism**. The priests accuse Nefertiti. But Pharaoh Akhenaten—the Living God—has spoken.

Akhenaten has decided that Thebes has too many reminders of the old gods. He has ordered a new capital—the City of the Sun—to be built many miles away.

* * *

A stonecutter from Thebes has worked long months on the city. Today, his wife and children will leave their home to join him in the City of the Sun. The children can't wait to begin. This will be their first trip outside Thebes. They are excited about the sights they will see. Their mother sees only the long and dusty journey ahead.

In the palace, other children are equally excited about the move, but their trip will be much more pleasant. Even now, Akhenaten, Nefertiti, and their three young daughters are climbing into their

People and Terms to Know

monotheism (MAHN•uh•THEE•iz•uhm)—belief in only one god or supreme being. Belief in many gods is called *polytheism*.

chariots. So are the court's nobles and politicians. They all move through the dusty streets toward the royal barge. The horses' hooves are stirring great clouds of dust. The mighty Nile River will carry them to their promised new home—the City of the Sun—**Akhetaten**.

* * *

A new dawn has come. Five years have passed. The bright disk of Aten appears between the twin hills for which the city is named—Akhetaten, "the horizon of Aten." Slowly, Aten extends his arms, offering the gift of life to the city and the green and gold croplands along the shores of the Nile.

In their royal chariot, Akhenaten and Nefertiti race past large homes surrounded by trees and sparkling pools. They ride to the temple where they will perform the morning ritual to the sun. Aten's rays leap from the gold and jewels in their crowns. Artists and stoneworkers, already at work on the city's great monuments, are momentarily blinded. In

---

People and Terms to Know

Akhetaten (AH•keh•TAH•tehn)—city built by Akhenaten to honor the god of the sun. See the map on page 41. Today, the site of Akhetaten is called Tel el-Amarna. The reign of Akhenaten is often called the "Period of Amarna."

▲
Nefertiti worships the sun in this limestone carving.

the time of the old gods, pharaohs were rarely seen by ordinary people. In the City of the Sun, Akhenaten is seen often with his wife and family.

In the lush, colorful gardens of the palace, the royal daughters play hide and seek. When their parents return from the temple, the family enjoys a meal of fruit and several different breads. Musicians play for their entertainment. As they eat, artists record the scene.

Akhenaten has changed not only the way people worship, but also the way people see their pharaoh. He changed the art of the times. Gone are the images of the pharaoh in battle. Gone are the threatening images of beastlike gods. Gone are the stone carvings and paintings of an expression-less king, his features shaped in the Egyptian idea of perfection.

Akhenaten orders his artists and sculptors to show the royal family as they really are. Colors are bright and features are life-like. Sometimes, the image is not

Akhenaten orders his artists and sculptors to show the royal family as they really are.

flattering. This new art shows the pharaoh playing with his daughters and holding his beautiful wife. Nefertiti is drawn equal in size to her husband.

Later in the day when the children are resting, Nefertiti poses for the royal sculptor and his students. They work hard to do justice to the queen's great beauty in their sculpture.

In the heat of the afternoon, Akhenaten seeks out the peace and quiet of his room to work on his great Hymn to the Sun:

Your dawning is beautiful in the horizon of heaven,
O living Aten, Beginning of life!
When you rise in the eastern sky,
You fill every land with your beauty;
For you are beautiful, great, glittering,
High over the earth;
Though you are afar, your rays are on earth;
Though you are on high, your footprints are the day.

Later in the hymn, Akhenaten thanks Aten for a long life for himself and his beloved Nefertiti. Neither will come to pass. After only seventeen years as pharaoh, Akhenaten dies. Nefertiti disappears from the pages of history. Within a few years, the young pharaoh, Tutankhaten, changes his name to **Tutankhamen**, brings back the old gods, and returns the capital to Thebes.

People and Terms to Know

Tutankhamen (TOOT•ahng•KAH•muhn)—Egyptian pharaoh who ruled from about 1333 to 1323 B.C., from the age of about nine until he died at eighteen. This was the King Tut of history whose tomb, discovered in 1922, contained hundreds of treasures of ancient Egypt.

Today, only the ruins of the City of the Sun remain. There stand unfinished statues and monuments of the king and his queen. Akhenaten's mummy and the mummy of Nefertiti have never been found.

QUESTIONS TO CONSIDER

1. Why were the priests angry with Akhenaten?

2. According to Akhenaten, what kind of god was Aten?

3. How was Akhenaten's worship of Aten different from the earlier Egyptian religion?

4. How were Akhenaten's and Nefertiti's values reflected in the art of their time?

5. If you had lived in Thebes when Akhenaten became pharaoh, how would you have felt about the changes he made?

Growing Up in Ancient Egypt
by Rosalie David

Rosalie David gives an entertaining, informative picture of what life was like in ancient Egypt.

Gods and Pharaohs
from Egyptian Mythology
by Geraldine Harris

Geraldine Harris uses myth, legend, and history to create an account of Egyptian civilization from its beginnings to its decline.

Pharaohs of Ancient Egypt
by Elizabeth Payne

Elizabeth Payne gives an introduction to ancient Egyptian civilization and religious beliefs. She also presents accounts of important pharaohs and their achievements, including those of Akhenaten.

An Ethiopian Tale: The Queen of Sheba

BY STEPHEN CURRIE

Dearest Mother,

How I long to speak to you! As a mere slave, of course, I have never learned to read and write. But here at the palace of the **queen of Sheba**, I see the scribes writing, writing, writing, and I wish I could do the same! If I could only write, I could tell you all the news and all that I think about. Because I cannot, I must write letters to you the only way I know how—in my head. It may be that if I think very hard, my ideas will fly over the Red Sea to you.

People and Terms to Know

queen of Sheba—ruler of an ancient land that probably covered present-day Ethiopia in Africa and present-day Yemen in the Arabian Peninsula as well. She was known for her wisdom and wealth.

Solomon and Sheba are shown meeting each other in a 20th-century
Ethiopian painting.

I am often lonesome here in **Ethiopia**. But serving the queen of Sheba is never dull. Her majesty is always thinking, always doing, always wondering. Even when we slaves are brushing her hair or helping to put on her robes, her brain is whirling. Today she asked me what fits inside a human head and yet is bigger than the universe. Her answer? Wisdom!

Your loving Daughter

Dearest Mother,

Writing these letters in my head has helped me feel closer to you. I miss our home in Arabia and I miss you terribly. Ethiopia is strange, with its mountains, its rain, and its green grasses. Still, the people are kind, and the queen of Sheba herself is an amazing person. This morning I was helping our queen to her throne room. There she would receive an ambassador from the court of **King Solomon** in Israel. When we reached the door, she asked if

---

People and Terms to Know

Ethiopia (EE•thee•OH•pee•uh)—country in east central Africa.

King Solomon—king of Israel during the tenth century B.C. Rich and the leader of a large and powerful empire, Solomon is probably best known for his wisdom. The phrase "wise as Solomon" is still common today.

I knew what was brighter than the sun, quicker than lightning, and stronger than a cyclone. I could not tell. She said it was the sudden flash of understanding that comes with wisdom. Do you know, I almost understood what she was saying?!

Your loving Daughter

Dearest Mother,

Such news! The queen is taking a journey to visit King Solomon himself! His riches are as great as those of our queen. His wisdom is as deep as hers. Did you know that Solomon has seven hundred wives? So they say!

The queen asked me who was lonelier than a woman with no husband. (I wondered if she was talking about herself. She has never found a man to equal her wealth and brain.) I gave up. She smiled and said, a man with seven hundred wives. I was confused at first. But then I realized that one may have seven hundred wives but none special enough to love and to be loved by in return.

I dread another voyage on the Red Sea. Journeying from Arabia to Ethiopia was enough for one lifetime! Still, I must admit that I am excited to

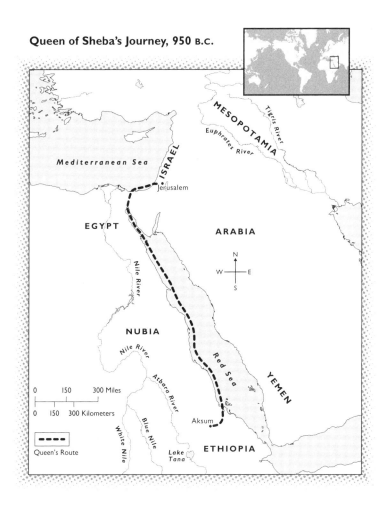

Queen of Sheba's Journey, 950 B.C.

Mediterranean Sea

MESOPOTAMIA

Euphrates River

Tigris River

ISRAEL

Jerusalem

EGYPT

ARABIA

N
W   E
S

Nile River

NUBIA

Nile River

Red Sea

YEMEN

Atbara River

0   150   300 Miles

0   150   300 Kilometers

Aksum

White Nile

Blue Nile

Lake Tana

ETHIOPIA

- - - -
Queen's Route

see Solomon. He has built himself a mighty empire, or so I am told. The queen says his country runs as smoothly as the sun on its way across the desert sands. We shall see, Mother!

Your loving Daughter

Dearest Mother,

At long last, the ship has docked and we are safely in Israel. Not a minute too soon—my stomach has not been the same since we left Africa behind. I wish you were here to stroke my head and sing to me. But I shall have to content myself with talking to you in this way.

The land of Solomon is most magnificent. The country looks much more like home than like the land of Sheba—sand and rock. The great man has over a thousand chariots and twelve thousand brave horsemen. The buildings stretch to the horizon! At present, the queen and Solomon are discussing trade routes, which is as dull as a camel's coat. I suspect that she has actually come to test his wisdom, and to let him test hers. This morning her majesty asked me what two things could meet with neither moving a muscle. When I gave up, she told me. It was the meeting of two minds. Hmm! I wonder whose minds she may be thinking of!

Your loving Daughter

Dearest Mother,

I *knew* that trade routes were not the reason for this visit! Solomon and her majesty spent this morning asking riddles. Our queen asked him many of the same riddles she has been asking me. But she did not ask what was lonelier than a woman with no husband.

Afterward, the queen seemed very thoughtful. What, she asked as I prepared her for bed, was more brilliant than jewels, more dazzling than beauty, and more precious than wisdom?

Love, she told me when I gave up. Love.

Your loving Daughter

Dearest Mother,

What excitement! Yesterday evening, King Solomon said he was wiser than our queen. And he offered her a challenge to prove it. Walk along the road outside the palace without touching the ground, he told her. If she could do it, he would give her a thousand bars of gold. If she could not, she would need to marry him!

Our queen accepted the challenge. She asked Solomon for his largest chariot and a team of his best stallions. As the horses galloped down the road, she walked briskly back and forth in the chariot. Truly, she met the challenge. Solomon had no choice but to give her the gold.

I only wonder why she seems so sad this morning.

Your loving Daughter

Dearest Mother,

Another challenge! Today Solomon offered her majesty five thousand bars of gold if she could sing a song that no one could hear. The penalty for failure, again, was to marry him. Our queen took his challenge. This time she called for Solomon's horsemen. Thousands came on their horses and stood before the palace gates. Then she commanded them to beat their swords upon their shields. The noise was more than anyone could stand. We all fled, moaning, with our hands over our ears. As we did, Sheba sang. No one could hear her because of the banging. Once again, she had won!

And yet I thought I heard her weeping last night.

Your loving Daughter

Dearest Mother,

Tonight over dinner Solomon made his third and final challenge. Before the night was over, he told her, she would take something that belonged to him. If she did, then she would have to marry him on the spot. If she did not, then he would give her ten thousand bars of gold—and never again ask for her hand in marriage.

Sheba told him that she was not a thief. She accepted the challenge.

Oh, Mother! I hope—I hope—oh, I do not know *what* I hope!

Your loving Daughter

▲
Servants prepare for the royal banquet.

Dearest Mother,

Last night at a royal banquet, Solomon served our queen spicy meats that burned the throat. After the meal she went to her bedchamber. I brushed her hair while she sat on the bed, near the bowl of water Solomon's servants had placed for her. Her eyes seemed far away.

When we were done, I crept onto my own sleeping mat. I thought of the challenge. What could she take? What would she want? Nothing, so far as I could tell.

I lay awake for some time. At some point I heard the queen stirring. By the light of the candle, I saw her touch her burning throat. She reached for the water dipper and drank long and deeply. Then she slept, and so did I.

In the morning the king entered the chambers, smiling broadly. He had won, he said. I could not see how, until he pointed to the water bowl. The water was gone. She had taken his water!

So our queen will now be a married woman, the wife of the wise and wealthy king of Israel. It will be a wonderful marriage, I am sure, for he loves her. And she loves him as well. Indeed, she is perhaps even wiser than he, although he won the final challenge.

I know this because of something she said tonight as I brushed out her hair. Even if not for the water, she told me, she still would have lost the challenge. For she had indeed taken something that belonged to him.

"What was it?" I asked, pausing as I brushed. Her smile was wise and beautiful. She had stolen his heart, she told me.

Your loving Daughter

*   *   *

According to legend, Sheba and Solomon married and had a son, Menelik. All Ethiopian kings claim to be descended from him.

QUESTIONS TO CONSIDER

1. Why might Sheba and Solomon's marriage have made good sense for their kingdoms?

2. How does the ability to ask and answer questions show wisdom?

3. If you were in the queen of Sheba's place, how would you have found out if Solomon was really wise?

Primary Source

The Queen's Quest

In an ancient book called *The Glory of Kings*, the queen of Sheba tells her people why she is going.

" 'Let My voice be heard by all of you, my people. I am going in search of Wisdom and Learning. Learning is better than treasures of silver and gold.'

"And so the Queen set out with much ceremony and splendor and gladness, her trust in God."

King Solomon and His Magic Ring
by Elie Wiesel

Nobel Peace Prize-winner Elie Wiesel retells many of the most famous tales about King Solomon from the Hebrew Bible and other Jewish writings.

King Solomon and the Queen of Sheba
by Blu Greenberg

Blu Greenberg uses both Jewish and Ethiopian traditions to retell the famous love story of King Solomon and the Queen of Sheba.

A Glorious Past:
Ancient Egypt, Ethiopia, and Nubia
by Ernestine Jenkins

Ernestine Jenkins presents the history of these African civilizations from ancient times to the Middle Ages.

The Fertile
Crescent

four

King Sargon and the Curse of Agade

BY MARIANNE McCOMB

Listen, grandchildren. Listen while I tell you the story of the most beautiful city in the world and the king who was foolish enough to destroy it. No, it's not a city that I lived in, and it's not a king whom I ever knew. But listen. My great-grandmother told me this story. She heard it from her grandmother, who heard it from a grandmother before that. So you see, children, this is a very, very old story about a man and a place that existed long ago.

Here is what my grandmother told me about the king, whose name was **Sargon**. When Sargon

---

People and Terms to Know

Sargon (SAHR•gahn)—Mesopotamian military leader and king who ruled from about 2335 to 2279 B.C. Sargon was the first to unite all Mesopotamia under one ruler. His empire also reached beyond Mesopotamia. See the map on page 73.

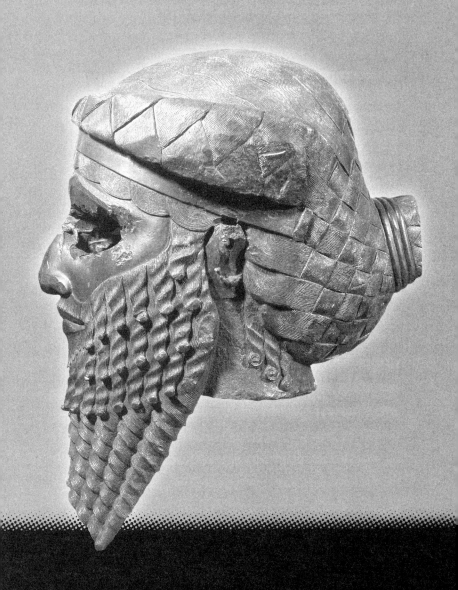

Sargon created the world's first empire around 2300 B.C.

was a baby, his mother placed him in a basket and sent him down the **Euphrates River**. He was rescued by a palm grower who lived in northern **Sumer**. The palm grower adopted Sargon and raised him as his own son.

According to legend, Sargon met the beautiful but deadly goddess **Ishtar** when he was a young man. Ishtar saw how handsome Sargon was and fell in love with him. As the daughter of the sky god Anu (AY•noo), she was used to having anything she wanted. Right there on the spot, she decided she wanted Sargon. So she told him that he would be her husband and that he would have to live with her in heaven.

But Sargon did not want to be married to this powerful goddess. He felt that he was cut out for better things. He wanted to stay on earth and be powerful in his own right. He was going to take over all the **city-states** from here to the Mediterranean

---

People and Terms to Know

Euphrates River (yoo•FRAY•teez)—river in southwest Asia. Today, it rises in Turkey, flows through Syria and Iraq, and eventually joins the Tigris River.

Sumer (SOO•muhr)—ancient region in the valley of the Euphrates River, north of its mouth.

Ishtar—in Sumerian legend, goddess of war, fertility, and love.

city-states—self-governing states, each made up of a single major city and the surrounding area.

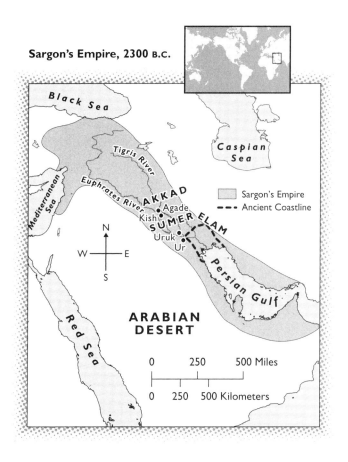

Black Sea

Caspian Sea

Tigris River

Euphrates River

AKKAD

Agade

Kish

SUMER ELAM

Uruk

Ur

Persian Gulf

Mediterranean Sea

N
W — E
S

ARABIAN DESERT

Red Sea

Sargon's Empire
Ancient Coastline

0   250   500 Miles
0   250   500 Kilometers

Sea, he explained to Ishtar. Then he would be king of the largest empire the world had ever known.

Ishtar was furious when Sargon said no to her. She almost killed him on the spot. But then she decided that it might be more fun to cause him trouble somewhere down the road. Also, she liked Sargon's plans to wage wars. Ishtar loved a good war.

So Ishtar gave Sargon some advice on how to conquer powerful city-states such as Uruk, Kish, and Ur. She also gave him an order. "When you've finished all your battles, build a capital city in the center of the empire," she said, "and name it Ishtar." Sargon promised he would do as she had asked. After all, he had no choice.

Grandchildren, you know that Sargon quickly became known as a brilliant but very cruel military leader. When he was still young, he went to work for King Ur-Zababa of Kish. Somehow, Sargon managed to overthrow Ur-Zababa and grab the throne of Kish for himself. From then on, there was no stopping him.

In the years that followed, King Sargon led his army from **Akkad** to defeat all of the city-states of Sumer and put them under his rule. Then he took control of Elam, which was east of the Tigris River. Next he marched toward the Mediterranean Sea, conquering many city-states along the way. Each time he conquered a new city-state, he declared it a part of his empire. He ordered all people of the region to begin speaking his tongue, which was known as Akkadian.

Eventually, Sargon ruled all the land between the rivers. Many of the conquered people hated

People and Terms to Know

Akkad (AK•ad)—ancient country in what is now Iraq.

Sargon. He took away their language and their kings and forced them to follow the ways of the Akkadians.

Of course, Sargon didn't care who hated him. In fact, he was so thrilled with his new empire that he decided to reward himself. He ordered his people to build a capital city for him. He told them to make it the most magnificent city the world had ever known.

Sargon ruled all the land between the rivers.

Hundreds of thousands of slaves spent years and years building Sargon's city. They created beautiful palaces, magnificent temples, and sturdy houses. They decorated many buildings with brightly painted tiles that glittered in the sun.

When the city was finished, Sargon knew he would have to give it a name. He remembered that Ishtar had ordered him to name it "Ishtar," but he hated that idea. He wanted everyone to know that it was *his* city. So he named it "Agade" so that everyone would know that it was a part of the Akkadian Empire, which he had created.

Our legend says that when Ishtar heard the name of the new city, she became furious. She decided to punish Sargon by hurting his new city. She sent down a curse on Agade! She proclaimed, "In Agade, the great fields and meadows will produce no grain. The fisheries will produce no fish. The watered gardens will produce neither honey nor wine."

Not long after, a terrible famine came to Agade. People in the city went hungry. The crops failed year after year, and the rivers and streams gave no fish. Thousands were hungry and homeless. Sargon's magnificent city was dying, and he could do nothing about it. The goddess Ishtar was much stronger than he.

A few years later, Sargon died. In Agade, things became even worse after his death. The rulers after Sargon tried to help, but it was no use. Ishtar's curse was too powerful. The city grew sicker and sicker. The people grew weaker and weaker. Many decided to leave their city. Even though the empire itself was not hurt by the curse, the city of Agade was ruined.

But my grandmother told me this, children, and I believe it to be the truth. She said that Sargon got what he deserved. He was too powerful, too cruel, and did not care about the lives and wishes of others. That's why he was punished by the gods.

Now let that be a lesson to you.

1. What three words would you use to describe King Sargon? Why?

2. According to the legend, what was the curse of Agade?

3. Why was King Sargon important in history?

The Story of Gilgamesh

BY WALTER HAZEN

A legend is a story often based on fact, but as it is passed down by word of mouth, it becomes larger than life. People throughout history have had their legends. The ancient Greeks and Romans created many such tales. The British had King Arthur. The early Americans took men such as Davy Crockett and John Henry and turned their stories into exciting legends. All peoples and nations have done the same.

The people of Sumer were no exception. Their most famous legendary hero was **Gilgamesh**.

People and Terms to Know

Gilgamesh (GIHL•guh•MEHSH)—legendary Sumerian king who was the hero of Sumerian and Babylonian tales. He was called "the Powerful, the Perfect, and the Wise."

This small bronze statue of a warrior in his chariot was made in ancient
Sumer around 2500 B.C.

Gilgamesh was a real king who ruled the Sumerian city-state of Uruk in about 2500 B.C.

The story of Gilgamesh is considered to be the first great **epic** of world literature. It was first written down around 2000 B.C. It tells about a great king's adventures and of his desire to live forever. It also gives us a glimpse of life in Mesopotamia some 4,000 years ago. Through the tale, we learn of the struggles of ancient peoples to understand and cope with the world in which they lived.

In the legend, Gilgamesh was described as two-thirds god and one-third human. He was tall, strong, and fearless in battle. He was also wise and very handsome. The women of Uruk loved him. This often made their husbands and male friends angry and jealous.

The jealous men of Uruk asked the goddess Ishtar to create a powerful rival to beat him. Ishtar agreed. She asked the lesser goddess Aruru (uh•ROO•roo) to take care of it. With a bit of clay and spit, Aruru created Enkidu (EN•kee•doo).

People and Terms to Know

epic—long poem or tale about the adventurous deeds of gods and heroes.

Enkidu was every bit as handsome and as wise as Gilgamesh. But there the similarity ended. Enkidu's body was covered with hair. He lived with the wild animals. He ate grass like the antelopes and drank with the beasts at the waterholes. People in the cities called him the "wild man."

Ishtar sent a beautiful girl to lure Enkidu into the city. When he arrived, he and Gilgamesh fought. They fought so hard that the earth shook for miles around. Enkidu was huge and had the strength of dozens of wild animals. Gilgamesh, however, proved his equal in every way. The fight continued for a long time. Gilgamesh finally won. After the fight, the two became good friends. And the longer they knew each other, the stronger their friendship grew.

Enkidu was huge and had the strength of dozens of wild animals. Gilgamesh, however, proved his equal in every way.

For a while, Gilgamesh and Enkidu enjoyed a life of lazy luxury. But they soon became bored. They decided to set out in search of adventure and excitement. Gilgamesh proposed that they go to the Great

Cedar Forest far away and cut down all of the cedar trees. He wanted to use the trees to build a cedar gate for the city.

The thought of entering the Great Cedar Forest bothered Enkidu. To do so, they would first have to fight its guardian monster, Humbaba (hoom•BAH•buh). Enkidu had seen the monster during his years of living in the wilds. He tried to get Gilgamesh to understand that it would be very foolish to challenge such a foe.

But Gilgamesh was determined. He and Enkidu entered the forbidden forest. And they *did* succeed in slaying the fire-breathing Humbaba. Then they cut down all the cedar trees and made a raft. They floated the raft down the Euphrates River to Uruk. There they watched over the building of a magnificent gate.

Gilgamesh's fame was now greater than ever. It was so great, in fact, that the goddess Ishtar fell in love with him. She offered him a golden chariot pulled by lions if he would marry her. But Gilgamesh said no. His rejection left her angry and bent on revenge.

Ishtar was determined to punish Gilgamesh. She returned to heaven and asked her father, the

▲

Humbaba, the monster that Gilgamesh and Enkidu killed. This sculpture of his head was carved in Babylonia around 700 B.C.

sky god Anu (AY•noo), for help. She begged Anu to create a fierce beast to kill Gilgamesh. When Anu at first refused, Ishtar said she'd destroy love throughout the universe. So Anu gave in and made a vicious bull known as the Bull of Heaven.

The Bull of Heaven was a fearsome sight. Its breath was so powerful that each time it breathed, huge cracks opened up in the earth. Hundreds of people fell to their deaths. Surely such a beast would make short work of Gilgamesh!

Or so Ishtar thought. With the help of Enkidu, however, Gilgamesh had little trouble killing the bull. When this happened, Ishtar was furious. She became even angrier when Enkidu ripped off one of the bull's legs and threw it in her face. That did it! Then she really punished Gilgamesh. Ishtar made Enkidu become sick and die.

Gilgamesh howled and wept. He grieved and mourned.

Gilgamesh howled and wept. He grieved and mourned. As he did so, he began to think, not just about Enkidu but also about death. He thought about his own death. He became aware that he, like Enkidu, would someday die. To avoid this fate, he began a long journey in search of eternal life. It was a journey in which he had to overcome many dangers.

After wandering for some time, Gilgamesh came to the island home of Utnapishtim (OOT•nah•PISH•tim). Utnapishtim, who was known as "the Faraway," was an immortal being who lived on an island paradise beyond the waters of death. In Mesopotamian mythology, he is like **Noah** of biblical fame. Utnapishtim told Gilgamesh of a great flood caused by the gods and how he had built a large boat to save his family and the animals of the earth. He also told Gilgamesh that when the flood was over, the gods had granted Utnapishtim and his wife eternal life.

When Utnapishtim finished his story of the flood, he told Gilgamesh the secret of eternal life. He said there was a certain plant at the bottom of the sea. If Gilgamesh found this plant and ate its fruit, he would live forever. Delighted, Gilgamesh tied stones to his feet and sank to the bottom of the ocean. He pulled the plant from the water and came to the surface.

If Gilgamesh found this plant and ate its fruit, he would live forever.

Gilgamesh did not immediately eat the fruit of the plant. He wanted to test it on some older man before trying it himself. So he set out on the long

People and Terms to Know

Noah—in the Bible, a man told by God to build an ark. This saved his family and one pair of each type of animal from a great flood that God caused to punish humans for being wicked.

journey back to Uruk. Along the way, however, a terrible thing happened. One day when Gilgamesh stopped to bathe, a snake crawled by and stole the magical plant. Gilgamesh returned home crushed. His search for eternal life was a failure.

QUESTIONS TO CONSIDER

1. What personal qualities do you think made Gilgamesh a great hero to the Sumerians?

2. What do you learn from the story about the gods and goddesses of ancient Sumer?

3. Which elements of the Gilgamesh legend do you think might be based on facts? Why?

4. What does this story tell you about the culture of ancient Sumer?

Gilgamesh the King
by Ludmila Zeman

Ludmila Zeman presents the epic adventures of the Mesopotamian hero Gilgamesh in a series of three books. In the first book, Gilgamesh and the wild man Enkidu first battle and then become friends.

The Revenge of Ishtar
by Ludmila Zeman

In book two, Gilgamesh and Enkidu overcome giants and monsters, but the angry goddess Ishtar causes Enkidu to die.

The Last Quest of Gilgamesh
by Ludmila Zeman

In the final book, Gilgamesh goes on a quest to find the secret of eternal life.

Tale of a Tablet House

BY STEPHEN FEINSTEIN

Ｉt was quiet in the classroom of the tablet house, a school for scribes in Sumer. And it was hot, as hot as an oven. In summertime, the lands along the banks of the Euphrates River baked beneath a broiling sun. The cooling rains wouldn't come until next winter. All of the students were hunched over their desks, carefully copying lists of words in the **cuneiform** script of Sumer. They wrote making wedge-shaped marks in a wet clay tablet with a special reed that had a triangular tip.

Twelve-year-old Akki stared at the clay tablet in front of him. He had only copied two of the words.

People and Terms to Know

cuneiform (KYOO•nee•uh•FAWRM)—ancient Mesopotamian form of writing. Cuneiform was the world's first form of writing. It was invented by Sumerian scribes around 3000 B.C.

Two scribes record the spoils from a victory in this Assyrian carving from around 800 B.C. The inset shows the wedge-shaped stylus (sharp-pointed writing instrument) and clay tablet used by a Mesopotamian scribe.

"I'm so tired of copying the same words over and over, day after day," he thought. His mind began to wander. Akki began daydreaming about his life in the days before he had been admitted to the tablet house. Akki wished that he could be outside working in the fields again alongside his father, Gamil. As they worked, his father would tell him tales of Gilgamesh and other heroes. The tales had been handed down from grandfather, to father, to son from earliest times.

> *"I'm so tired of copying the same words over and over, day after day."*

Those were happy times, indeed. Then, five years ago, his parents got different ideas. They did not want their only son to work in the fields all his life. They wanted more for their son. Akki should not have to live the rest of his life in a mud-brick hut. No, Akki would live and work in a palace, or a temple. He would get an education. He would become a scribe. And someday, he would be a wealthy man!

Akki's parents, Gamil and Puabi, knew that the students in the tablet house were from wealthy homes. They came from the families of rich merchants, government officials, or doctors. An education in the city of **Ur** cost a lot of money, more money than Gamil and Puabi had. They would have to save and sacrifice in order to send Akki to school. Gamil sold one of their two oxen. Puabi spent her evenings mending the neighbors' clothing. Amazingly, after a year, Gamil and Puabi had saved enough money to enroll Akki in the tablet house.

Akki had been very excited at the time. He had visions of himself dressed in the fancy robes of a royal scribe, writing down letters from the king of Ur. What fun he was going to have! Then, one morning, several days after he had entered the tablet house, Akki had a big surprise. As he turned around in his seat to answer a question from the student behind him, there was a loud crack! A flash of pain shot across Akki's back! Akki screamed out and looked up. There was the schoolmaster, Luga, glaring down at him, a long cane in his hand. "So this is how it's going to be," thought Akki, tears forming in his eyes. "What have I gotten myself into?"

People and Terms to Know

Ur—city of ancient Sumer, located on the Euphrates River.

As the months and years went by, Akki got used to the strict rules and harsh punishments of the tablet house. Akki wasn't the only student to feel the sting of the cane hitting him. Students were caned for failing to finish a lesson, for sloppy writing, or for dressing carelessly. They also were caned for not being on time in the morning, for giving wrong answers, and for talking in class. Akki was not happy at school, but he was becoming an educated young man. He had memorized several hundred cuneiform characters. He learned how to read and write. He copied whatever he was told to copy. But Akki no longer looked forward to becoming a scribe.

Students were caned for failing to finish a lesson, for sloppy writing, or for dressing carelessly.

So Akki daydreamed that afternoon in the hot classroom. Only the buzz of an insect going by disturbed the silence. Akki grew drowsy. His eyes closed, and he rested his head on his desk. Soon Akki was walking through the marshes near the Euphrates River. He stopped when he got to the riverbank. A white crane was standing there as still as a statue. Suddenly, Akki heard footsteps approaching behind him. The crane flew away with a cry. A cane slammed down across Akki's hands! He was back in the classroom—and there was schoolmaster Luga with his cane.

That night, Akki wrote a message to his parents on a clay tablet. They would have to get a scribe to read it to them because they could not read. Akki wrote, "Dear Mom and Dad, I can no longer stand the life here. Please allow me to return home a failure." But when he had finished writing, he knew he could not send the tablet to his parents. Gamil and Puabi, who had done so much for him, would be terribly disappointed. It would break their hearts. He could not do this to them, no matter how much he hated school. Akki rubbed out the message while the clay was still wet.

This clay tablet shows the wedge-shaped characters of cuneiform, probably the world's first system of writing. ▶

The next morning, before classes began, Akki ran into Ishar, one of the assistant teachers. Ishar was one of the few people at the tablet house whom Akki considered a friend. "Ishar," said Akki, "I don't know if I can continue along this path."

"Akki, not every scribe works for merchants or government officials. That sort of work is not for everyone."

"What do you mean, Akki?" asked Ishar. "I've never heard you talk like this before."

"I mean I cannot go on copying lists of merchants' sales or measurements of plots of land," said Akki. "It means nothing to me. It is all so boring. I'm afraid I will run away from school."

"Akki, I'm glad you told me this now. Don't do something you might regret for the rest of your life," said Ishar. "I have an idea, my friend. This might be just the thing for you."

Ishar told Akki about a special project that he and several of the other assistant teachers were working on. "Akki, not every scribe works for merchants or government officials. That sort of work is not for everyone. Some of us have more joyful work. We are writing down the poems and epics of our rich

Sumerian past. We want to make sure that our literature does not become lost to future Sumerians. If you're interested, I'll ask Luga if you can be assigned to work with us. What do you say?"

Akki stared at Ishar, a wide grin on his face. The idea that he could be a scribe and actually enjoy his work was beginning to sink in. He hadn't been this excited since his very first day at the tablet house. "Thank you, Ishar! Yes, of course I'm interested!" Akki finally blurted out.

That night, Akki wrote a different message to his parents. Ishar had gotten Luga's approval to include Akki in their special project. Akki was going to help them record the epic adventures of Gilgamesh, the greatest hero of Sumerian folklore! Akki told his parents all about the Gilgamesh project. And this time he made sure to send them the tablet.

QUESTIONS TO CONSIDER

1. Why did Akki's parents want their son to become a scribe?

2. Why was Akki unhappy at the tablet house?

3. Why didn't Akki send his parents the message asking permission to return home a failure?

4. How did Ishar propose to solve Akki's problem?

5. What does this story show about the importance of scribes in Sumerian society?

A True Story of a Scribe

We know about the schools for scribes and the scribes' lives from the many textbooks, essays, and letters that have been found on clay tablets. In one, probably written by a teacher, a pupil speaks:

"I recited my tablet, ate my lunch, prepared my new tablet, wrote it, finished it; and then they assigned me my oral work, and in the afternoon they gave me my written work. When school was over, I went home and found my father sitting there. I told my father of my written work, then read my tablet to him, and my father was delighted."

Mesopotamia and the Fertile Crescent
by Mavis Pilbeam and John Malam

Mavis Pilbeam and John Malam give an introduction to the civilizations of the ancient Near East. They explore their governments, laws, food, science and technology, arts and crafts, religions, and warfare.

Mesopotamia
by Pamela F. Service

Pamela F. Service gives an introduction to ancient Mesopotamian society and discusses its religious beliefs and cultural achievements.

Alphabetical Order:
How the Alphabet Began
by Tiphaine Samoyault

Tiphaine Samoyault describes how the first systems of picture writing, such as Mesopotamian cuneiform, developed into the letters of modern alphabets.

Hammurabi's Code

BY LYNNETTE BRENT

Adad (AY•dad) felt anxious as he scanned the horizon. The sun, now a deep shade of red, was sinking in the west. Night would soon fall. Adad hated the coming darkness. All last week, a robber had been in the area at night, stealing oxen and sheep.

"This is the worst possible time to lose any sheep," Adad thought. The city of **Babylon** was growing rapidly. Many people wished to buy the woolen cloth that Adad's wife, Siduri (sih•DOOR•ee), wove and sold at the marketplace. Adad was glad that his sheep pens were strongly built. Still, he thought that maybe tonight he should stay awake and listen for the thief.

People and Terms to Know

Babylon (BAB•uh•luhn)—capital of the ancient Babylonian Empire. It was located on the Euphrates River in southwest Asia.

Hammurabi had the 282 laws of his Code carved on this pillar. He is shown at the top standing in front of a god. The inset above shows the entire pillar.

The evening was warm, so Adad gathered his family to sleep on the roof. Soon the night breeze lulled the children to sleep. But Adad was on edge. Would the robber strike *him* tonight? He listened to every sound.

Later that night, Adad awoke to a strange banging sound. It was the wooden gate on the sheep pen! The gate was banging open and shut, open and shut. Had one of his sheep escaped? Adad raced down the stairs from the roof. He ran as quickly as he could without falling in the dark. He tried to keep quiet so that his hurried footsteps wouldn't alarm the family. He was too late! The gate was open and two sheep were gone. Someone had opened the gate.

Adad was on edge. Would the robber strike **him** *tonight? He listened to every sound.*

Adad sank to the ground, his head in his hands. He didn't know what he would tell Siduri. He sat awake until daybreak, saddened by the loss of two prize animals.

As the sun rose, Siduri stretched and looked at the sky. Today, she needed to go to the market. The market was always exciting and full of people. Siduri liked to watch the merchants from foreign lands selling their strange goods. Today, Siduri would sell some of her woven cloth and buy the day's food.

But then she noticed Adad checking on the animals. Was something wrong? Oh, no! Siduri suddenly realized—the thief had struck!

"Adad!" called Siduri. "How many are missing?"

"Two," he replied.

When Siduri reached the bottom of the stairs, she looked at Adad and sighed. "Oh, Adad! Do you really think we're better off living here in Babylon? When we lived outside the city, we didn't worry about robbers coming in the night!"

"Of course, we're better off here, Siduri," Adad said. "Any large city has problems. It's true that there's more crime here and we have to pay taxes. Those things are new to us. But we have more food than we ever had before. Our boys are going to school. And there are laws to protect us, thanks to our king, **Hammurabi**. If the person who stole our sheep is caught, we know that he'll have to pay us back. King **Hammurabi's Code** of laws is fair for everyone in the kingdom."

People and Terms to Know

Hammurabi (HAM•uh•RAH•bee)—king of the city-state of Babylon who ruled from about 1792 to 1750 B.C. Hammurabi conquered nearby city-states to create the Babylonian Empire, bringing all of Mesopotamia under one rule.

Hammurabi's Code—collection of 282 laws and edicts of the Babylonian Empire. Carved in stone, this code is the best-preserved legal document from an ancient civilization.

▲
This carving shows Hammurabi kneeling in worship.

"I guess you're right," Siduri agreed, "but it will be hard to get enough wool if two sheep are missing. Let's repair the pens before the other sheep get away."

Adad and Siduri worked harder than usual the next few days. They made as much cloth as they could. Because Babylon was on the Euphrates River, visitors going up and down the river stopped at the market. Adad and Siduri wanted to be sure that they had enough cloth to sell. They also had to keep a close eye on their livestock. Would the thief strike again?

The next week, they were surprised once more by loud noises in the middle of the night. Down the road, the thief was trying to make another getaway. But this time he didn't get very far. Trying to escape, he stumbled. He twisted his foot and fell headlong on the dusty road. Now he couldn't run away. Adad and his neighbors crowded around the struggling young man. They kept him from escaping until the guards arrived.

> *"Here in Babylon, we have a code to punish criminals. Our king, Hammurabi, was told by the gods to make a code of laws."*

The thief, a man named Hanish (HAH•neesh), tried to sputter his story to the guards. He had come to Babylon only a short time ago. He had no family. He had no trade. He was just trying to survive!

The guards were not sympathetic.

"You are a thief, just like any other," said Shullat (SHOOL•lat), the head guard. "Here in Babylon, we have a code to punish criminals. Our king, Hammurabi, was told by the gods to make a code of laws. That code is carved in stone and displayed in temples throughout the land. And we all follow that code."

"What does that mean for me?" asked Hanish anxiously.

"Your case is just like any other case of stealing. You stole from private citizens in our kingdom. Your sentence will be to repay each of those people ten times the value of what you stole."

"Ten times?!"

"Yes. Consider yourself lucky. Had you stolen from the palace, you would have had to pay thirty times the worth of the stolen goods."

"What happens if I cannot pay?"

"The code is very clear." Shullat looked stern. "If a thief cannot pay, he is put to death. And the government will pay the victims for their losses."

"No! It cannot be!" Hanish gulped. "Why are these laws so strict?"

"Hammurabi believes that people should be responsible for their actions. Many of the laws are based on a rule called 'an eye for an eye.' When a criminal commits an injury, then he is punished with the same injury. If a builder constructs a house and the house collapses and kills the owner, then the builder will be put to death. If a son hits his father, then the son's hand will be cut off. Hammurabi's Code also has rules about conducting business and about marriage and divorce."

Hanish felt a stab of terror. The only way to clear himself of his crimes was to repay the owners for all the livestock he had stolen. How could he raise that much money?

"An Eye for an Eye"

Hammurabi's Code not only dealt with crime, but also with marriage and the family, personal injury, and trade. Each law presents both a specific case and a punishment (if one is required). The following are some actual laws from Hammurabi's Code:

"If a man has been taken captive, and there is no food in his house, and his wife moves into the house of another man, then that woman bears no blame.

"If a man has destroyed the eye of another free man, his own eye shall be destroyed.

"If a man strikes the body of a man who is superior in rank, he shall publicly receive sixty lashes with a cowhide whip."

QUESTIONS TO CONSIDER

1. What was Hanish's crime? How would he be punished?

2. Which laws from Hammurabi's Code do you consider fair? Why?

3. Which laws do you consider unfair? Why?

4. What does this story tell you about life in Babylon?

5. What were some advantages and disadvantages of living in Babylon?

The Story of Ruth

**FROM THE BIBLE AS RETOLD BY
FITZGERALD HIGGINS**

The three widows—one old, two young—stood weeping at a crossroads as they said farewell. The old woman's name was Naomi (nay•OH•mee); the young women, Orpah (OR•puh) and Ruth, had been married to her sons. Naomi was from **Israel**; Orpah and Ruth were from **Moab**. Israel and Moab were neighboring countries on the southeastern shore of the Mediterranean Sea. The Israelites worshiped one God, but their neighbors worshiped many gods, and this sometimes led to wars. During

People and Terms to Know

Israel (IHZ•ree•uhl)—ancient kingdom of southwest Asia on the eastern shore of the Mediterranean Sea.
Moab (MOH•ab)—ancient kingdom east of the Dead Sea.

Boaz (on horseback) invites Ruth to collect grain from his fields.
This illustration was made around 1250 A.D., more than two thousand
years after the time of Ruth's story.

this period (sometime between 1220 and 1020 B.C.), the Israelites did not have kings, but were led by military rulers called **judges**.

Ten years earlier, Naomi and her husband and two sons had left Israel and moved to Moab because their own land was suffering from a terrible famine. Naomi's husband had later died, and her two sons, who had married Moabite women, had also died. Naomi now heard that the hungry years had passed back home, so she decided to return. Orpah and Ruth, who loved Naomi, wanted to go with her. Naomi loved her Moabite daughters-in-law, but she told them to stay in their own land and find new husbands among their own people. Orpah sorrowfully kissed Naomi good-bye and left, but Ruth refused to leave her.

"Your people shall be my people, and your God my God."

"Where you go," Ruth told Naomi, "I will go; where you live, I will live. Your people shall be my people, and your God my God."

Naomi saw that Ruth was determined to go with her. So the two women traveled together to

People and Terms to Know

judges—military rulers of ancient Israel between the time of Joshua and the establishment of the kingdom by Saul around 1020 B.C.

Naomi's home, **Bethlehem**. When they reached Bethlehem, everyone in town came out to greet them. The people asked, "Is this Naomi?"

But she replied, "Don't call me Naomi, call me Mara (MAH•ruh), for the Lord has dealt very bitterly with me." (The name Naomi means "sweetness"; the name Mara means "bitter.")

The people of Bethlehem were just beginning to harvest their grain. Naomi and Ruth were quite poor. So Ruth said to her mother-in-law, "Let me go out into the grainfields. Perhaps they will let me gather the grain dropped by the harvesters." Israelite law permitted poor people to get food for themselves by gathering the grain dropped by the harvesters. This was called "gleaning." In fact, farmers were required to leave a part of the harvest to be gleaned by the poor. Naomi agreed with Ruth's plan. So Ruth went and gleaned in the field after the harvesters had done their work.

Naomi had a rich **kinsman** named Boaz. Ruth had just reached the fields belonging to Boaz when he arrived and noticed her.

People and Terms to Know

Bethlehem (BETH•luh•hem)—ancient town in Israel on the west bank of the Jordan River south of Jerusalem. See the map on page 16.

kinsman—male relative; member of the same extended family or clan.

He asked his servant, "To whom does this young woman belong?"

The servant replied, "She is the Moabite woman who came back with Naomi from Moab. She has been working hard since early this morning."

Boaz approached Ruth and said, "Stay and glean in my fields. No one will bother you. If you are thirsty, go and drink from the water jars my harvesters use. I have heard how well you have cared for your mother-in-law—even leaving your homeland to come here with her. May the Lord reward you for your good deeds."

So Ruth stayed all day in Boaz's fields. At midday he invited her to eat with his harvesters. When Ruth got home that evening, Naomi was delighted to hear what had happened.

"My daughter," Naomi said to Ruth, "I need to provide for your future. Boaz is our kinsman and he clearly likes you. Here's what you should do. Wash and perfume yourself, put on your best clothes, and visit him tonight when he's through threshing the grain. Wait until he's finished eating and drinking, and then sit down beside him. If I'm not mistaken about his feelings for you, he will take over from there."

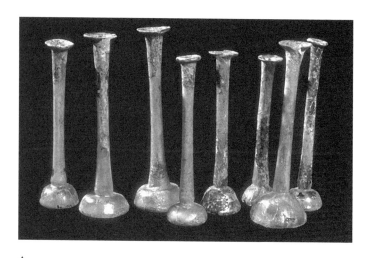

Ruth may have used a perfume bottle like these, which were found in graves from ancient Israel.

Naomi hoped that Boaz would want to marry Ruth. If a married man died without a son—as Ruth's husband had—Israelite custom required his nearest male relative to marry his widow and provide him with a son.

Ruth agreed to follow her mother-in-law's advice and everything happened as Naomi had foreseen. Boaz finished his work, had something to eat and drink, and lay down peacefully to sleep on a heap of grain. Ruth came in quietly and sat down next to him. About midnight, Boaz woke up suddenly and was startled to find a woman beside him.

"Who are you?" he asked.

"I am Ruth, your servant. I seek your protection, for you are my kinsman."

Boaz was pleased and replied, "Here is another example of your loyalty to your family. You preferred an older kinsman like me instead of some young fellow. I want to marry you, Ruth, for everyone knows you are a good woman. But you have another kinsman who has a better right to marry you than I do. If he is willing to give up his claim, then I will make you my wife."

The next day, Boaz went to the town gate. No sooner had he got there than the other kinsman, of whom he had spoken to Ruth, arrived. Boaz first asked this man to come and sit down. Next he gathered ten men from the city to serve as witnesses and asked them to sit down as well. In front of these witnesses, he asked his kinsman whether he wanted to marry Ruth. The man said no, he could not afford to, and asked Boaz to marry her. Boaz agreed. Then the man took off his sandal and handed it to Boaz in front of

"I am Ruth, your servant. I seek your protection, for you are my kinsman."

the witnesses. Boaz accepted it. According to Israelite custom, this sealed the bargain. All the people rejoiced for Boaz and Ruth.

So Boaz and Ruth were married, and in time Ruth had a son. All of the neighborhood women rejoiced with Naomi, telling her that the Lord had not forgotten her in her old age. Naomi took the child and held him and became his nurse. The women named the child Obed (OH•bed). When he grew up, he became the father of Jesse, who in turn was the father of Israel's greatest king, **David**.

QUESTIONS TO CONSIDER

1. Why is it important in this story that Naomi is from Israel and Ruth is from Moab?

2. How did ancient Israelite custom provide for the feeding of the poor?

3. How did the duties of kinsmen help protect widows in ancient Israel?

4. What kinds of feelings do Ruth and Boaz have for each other?

5. What do you think this story is saying about how we should treat outsiders?

6. What is your opinion of Ruth's decision to go with her mother-in-law and leave her homeland?

People and Terms to Know

David—(died c. 962) second king of Israel and traditional author of many of the Psalms in the Bible.

Ancient India
and China

Mohenjo-Daro: A Mystery

BY DEE MASTERS

Pakistan, 1987 A.D.

Huan (hyoo•AHN) looked down into the pit. The man at the bottom held up a large dirt-covered bone.

"Hey," Huan called. "What's that?"

The man in the pit looked up, surprised. "A mandible," the man said.

"A jawbone? That's a pretty big jawbone! I'd stay out of that guy's way, Dr. Dani." The doctor was an **archaeologist** on the research project that Huan's father was with this summer.

People and Terms to Know

archaeologist (AHR•kee•AHL•uh•jist)—scientist who studies ancient civilizations.

This photograph of the ruins of Mohenjo-Daro shows the Great Bath (left foreground) and the fort (right rear).

"It's from an elephant," said Dr. Dani. "About 3,000 years ago the people here in the **Indus River Valley** hunted elephants."

"My Dad told me it was wetter then," Huan said. "He has been keeping me up on this dig." Huan looked up into the cloudless sky. "I wish it was cooler now. It's too hot."

The doctor scooped up some dirt and carefully dropped it in a fine mesh screen box. The screen would separate the **artifacts** from the soil. "Well, it's going to be at least 110 degrees today, easily."

The doctor picked a piece of pottery out of the screen box. Huan saw something else. "What's that dark blue thing in the corner of the box?" he asked.

"It looks like a **lapis lazuli** bead," the doctor said. He held it up to Huan. "Here, put it in the plastic bag. We'll add it to our records tonight."

Huan took the red clay pottery and the lapis bead. He looked farther up the sloping, 50-foot-high mound to where men were uncovering an ancient sewer. "There's not much here now. It really

---

People and Terms to Know

Indus River Valley—wide valley made by the Indus River in present-day Pakistan. One of the world's earliest civilizations developed here.

artifacts—objects remaining from early civilizations. Even broken pieces of artifacts interest archaeologists.

lapis lazuli (LAP•ihs LAZ•uh•lee)—dark blue, semiprecious stone used for jewelry.

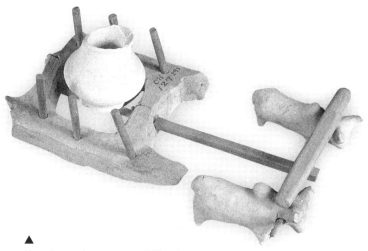

▲

Four thousand years ago, a child in the
Indus Valley may have played with this tiny
cart drawn by two young bulls.

looks like its name: Mohenjo-Daro, 'the mound
of the dead.' What did the people who lived here
call it?"

"We don't know," the archeologist replied. "It's
really a mystery city. But we've uncovered a lot of
the mystery."

Looking closely at the pottery in his hand, Huan
said, "There is writing on the **shard**."

Dr. Dani was now on all fours in the pit. He took
a small brush to clean dirt away from another find.
"Yes," he said. "I can tell your father is an archaeologist. Not many fourteen-year-olds would know
the word *shard*."

People and Terms to Know

shard—broken piece of pottery.

"What does the writing say?" asked Huan.

Dr. Dani stopped working and laughed, "We don't know."

"Well, what happened to all the people who lived here?" Huan continued.

"We don't know," the doctor said, still smiling. "But we have a few guesses."

"The writing on the shard is some of the earliest writing in the world."

"Cool," Huan grinned. "You guys don't know much about this place at all."

"Right," the doctor admitted. "But we know that in about 2600 B.C., there was a city of more than forty thousand people here. Also, we do know that this was one of the earliest cities anywhere and probably the first city laid out in blocks like most modern cities. The writing on the shard is some of the earliest writing in the world."

"OK, enough," said Huan. "How about this lapis bead?"

"That's easier," replied the archaeologist. "See this five-inch <u>terra cotta</u> statue?"

"Looks like a goddess," Huan said.

People and Terms to Know

terra cotta—baked clay pottery.

"Could be. We don't know. There are a lot of them here. It might have been a little girl's doll. But look at all the necklaces on it. The women wore a lot of jewelry."

The doctor kept talking. But Huan's imagination, helped by information he remembered from his father's letters, took over. He stared at the dark blue bead in his hand. The doctor's voice faded out.

Mohenjo-Daro, 2600 B.C.
Thousands of years earlier

Huan saw himself as a young man wearing a mask made from the white feathers of a beautiful river bird. The young man used the mask to sneak up on another river bird and catch it. He ran quickly to the main gate of his red brick city. He was proud to live here. His city was the largest in the Indus River valley. Today, though, he was in a hurry. A parade honoring a merchant slowed him down. Normally, he would have stopped to watch the **zebu** bulls pulling the merchants' carts. Zebus were very big and very smart. When the driver called "left!" they turned left!

People and Terms to Know

zebu (ZEE·boo)—large ox used for transportation and plowing.

The young man ran up the straight streets. The whole town was built on a hill. Even so, the young man knew the river could destroy his city when the floods came in the **monsoon** season. The city had already been washed away four times. But, if the river changed its course and flowed somewhere else, the town wouldn't be there. It was the river valley's rich soil that made their farm yields so great. It was the traders that came by boat that made their markets hum. But because of the flooding river, no one built big expensive buildings. Personal jewelry and small statues could be easily saved in flood time.

The young man knew the river could destroy his city when the floods came in the monsoon season.

The young man passed the lower-class houses and entered the twenty-foot-high, walled section of the city where members of his Rhino Clan lived in their three-room brick homes. The wall wasn't built to keep enemies out. They didn't have any enemies. They traded with everyone, and everyone needed them to be there to help trade run smoothly. The walls were to keep out the floodwaters.

People and Terms to Know

monsoon—wind system that brings very heavy summer rains to southern Asia.

The young man raced past the great public bathing pool. It was 39 feet long, 23 feet wide, and 8 feet deep. It was a favorite gathering place for the entire city. Today, though, he ran past the pool and carried the beautiful river bird to the top of a three-story house. There, under a shade porch, the northern men were trading their lapis and **turquoise** for his city's wheat and cotton cloth.

He showed them the long white river bird feathers. He traded them for enough lapis to finish the blue necklace he had been working on for so long. The stones were just right. They were the color of the night sky. He would cut small holes in these stones and string them on a necklace. Then he would give it to the young woman who would be his wife. Their parents had arranged their marriage when they were born. This would be the first man's-gift he would give her.

Pakistan, 1987 A.D.

"Toilets." The voice of Dr. Dani broke into the daydream. "They had great plumbing. All the houses had toilets with wooden seats."

People and Terms to Know

turquoise—semiprecious blue-green stone used for jewelry.

"What?" Huan said.

"Toilets," Dr. Dani said. Then he noticed that Huan was still looking at the lapis bead. "You look very interested in that."

Huan was interested. He knew what the young man who had lived three thousand years before would have liked. He would have wanted Huan to give that dark blue lapis bead with the small hole in it to the girl with the black hair who always got the highest grade in his history class. He sighed. You can't take artifacts for souvenirs, even if a voice from the past whispers.

QUESTIONS TO CONSIDER

1. What is known about Mohenjo-Daro?

2. What is mysterious about Mohenjo-Daro?

3. How are the archaeologists trying to get clues to understand Mohenjo-Daro?

4. What clues does the story provide to understanding the disappearance of Mohenjo-Daro?

Life of the Buddha

BY STEPHEN FEINSTEIN

Q ueen Mahamaya awoke with a start! She had been dreaming—a wonderful dream that had filled her with happiness. The dream was so clear that it had seemed real, and she remembered many of its details. There had been a great silvery elephant with six tusks! It had brought her a white lotus flower with a jewel in its center. The elephant had come up close to her and touched her right side. But Mahamaya had not been afraid. She wondered what the strange dream could mean.

Mahamaya ran through the palace to find her husband, King Suddhodhana. When she told him about her dream, he grew excited. He called the wisest **Brahmans** in all of Kapilavastu to his palace.

People and Terms to Know

Brahmans (BRAH•muhnz)—Hindu priests who served the creator god Brahma.

Head of the Buddha carved around 250 B.C.

Word went out from his kingdom in the foothills of the Himalayas. When the priests arrived, Suddhodhana described the queen's dream. He asked the priests to interpret it. They held a brief discussion.

Persons and Places in the Story

Mahamaya (MAH•huh•MY•yuh)
Siddhartha's mother.

Suddhodhana
(SOOD•doh•DAH•nah)
Siddhartha's father.

Kapilavastu
(KUHP•ee•lah•VUHS•tu)
Siddhartha's birthplace.

Yasodhara (YA•so•DAH•rah)
Siddhartha's wife.

Chandaka (chan•DAH•kah)
Siddhartha's charioteer.

Rahula (ruh•HOO•luh)
Siddhartha's son.

Sarnath (sahr•NAT)
place of Buddha's first sermon.

"Your Highness, Queen Mahamaya will give birth to a son, a young prince destined for greatness!" said one of the priests. "He will become the next king of Kapilavastu, if he so chooses. However, should he go forth into the world beyond the royal palace, he will find the Truth. The whole world will then benefit from his wisdom."

The king and queen were filled with joy upon hearing the priest's words. But later, when his excitement had worn off, Suddhodhana remembered the part about their son's finding the Truth. The more he thought about this, the less he liked it. Many times, in his travels, Suddhodhana had met seekers of the Truth. They were holy men who wandered up and down the length of India. They begged for their food and never stayed long in one place. King Suddhodhana did not wish to see his son follow in their footsteps. He would do whatever he could to shelter his son from the outside world.

When Mahamaya gave birth, she did indeed have a son. There was rejoicing throughout the kingdom. Suddhodhana and Mahamaya named their son

<u>Siddhartha Gautama</u>. Visitors began to arrive from all parts of the kingdom to see the young prince.

Soon after the celebrations in the kingdom ended, however. The royal palace was filled with sadness. Mahamaya had become ill and died. Her sister then agreed to look after Siddhartha. She loved the young prince as if he were her own son. The king adored the boy. He took pride in the fact that someday Siddhartha would rule the kingdom in his place. He hired the best teachers in the kingdom for Siddhartha. The young prince was very bright and soon learned everything his teachers knew. The boy then taught his teachers some things they hadn't known.

The young prince was especially fond of animals. One day, while Siddhartha was in the garden, some swans flew overhead. Suddenly, one of them fell to the ground next to him. Siddhartha bent down and looked at the bird. There was an arrow sticking into it. Siddhartha removed the arrow and walked toward the palace, cradling the injured swan in his arms.

"Where are you going with my swan?" cried an angry voice. Siddhartha turned and saw his cousin.

People and Terms to Know

Siddhartha Gautama (sid•DAHR•tuh GOW•tuh•muh)— (563–483 B.C.) the Buddha, Indian philosopher and founder of Buddhism. In the Sanskrit language, "Siddhartha" means "he who will accomplish." Today, over 340 million people in the world are Buddhist.

"Give me the swan. He is mine. I shot him with my bow and arrow."

Siddhartha refused to hand over the swan. It was left to the judges of the royal court to decide who should get the swan. The judges ruled in favor of Siddhartha. "The swan should belong to the one who saved its life," they said, "not to the one who tried to take its life."

When he turned sixteen, Siddhartha was married to Yasodhara, a beautiful young princess. King Suddhodhana gave a splendid wedding feast for the young couple. As a wedding gift, he gave them three new palaces. They stood within a park that had gardens, fountains, and many trees. The king hoped that Siddhartha would be so happy there that he would never go away from home. At first Siddhartha *was* very happy, spending many hours with his wife in their beautiful gardens. Often musicians and dancers entertained them.

Thirteen years went by. Siddhartha, now twenty-nine, had become restless. One day he asked his charioteer, Chandaka, to take him riding beyond the palace gates. They had gone only a short distance when they saw an old man by the side of the road. He was thin as a rail and leaned on a wooden cane. His cheeks were sunken in his wrinkled face. The few hairs on his head were white, and he had no teeth. Siddhartha asked the charioteer what was wrong with the man.

"Old age," replied Chandaka. "It is what happens to all of us."

As they continued on their way, they came upon a sick man lying on the ground. He was doubled up in pain. "That poor man is very sick," said Chandaka.

Siddhartha was lost in thought. He had never thought about suffering before.

They continued traveling. Late in the day, they encountered a funeral procession. A dead man was wrapped in a white sheet. People were about to **cremate** the body. Family members were moaning and crying in sorrow. "We all die, sooner or later," said Chandaka.

Siddhartha was lost in thought. He had never thought about suffering before. He wondered how people could ever be happy, knowing that they all faced old age, sickness, and death.

The next day, he went riding again with Chandaka. This time they came upon a holy man

---

People and Terms to Know

cremate—reduce a dead body to ashes by burning.

wearing a long robe colored with the yellow-orange dye made from the saffron plant. He was begging for food. The holy man told them that he had given up all of his belongings. He had left the people he was close to. He was on a journey to look for the Truth—the secret of life over death. Siddhartha realized that this was the path he must follow. Now that he knew there was so much suffering in the world, he could no longer be happy. To find the Truth, to find peace, he would have to leave everyone and everything dear to him—his wife, his father, and his palaces.

Siddhartha announced his plan to leave his old life behind. The king was filled with sorrow but could do nothing to stop him. On the day of Siddhartha's departure, his wife gave birth to a baby boy. They named the child Rahula. Had the child been born slightly earlier, it would have been the most exciting day in Siddhartha's life. But now, Siddhartha was determined to leave. Nothing, not even the birth of his son, could change his mind.

For the next six years, Siddhartha wandered through forests and over mountains. He followed the **Ganges River** and crossed the hot dusty plains of India. Early in his travels, he had given up his palace clothes and put on the saffron-colored robe of a holy man. He got a bowl to use for begging. Whenever he met a wandering holy man, he would ask him about the Truth and how to find it. But none could answer his questions.

Next, Siddhartha sought out Brahman priests. He studied with them and learned all of their prayers and rituals. But the priests could not explain how to end suffering. Siddhartha then went for long periods denying his body food and comfort. Sometimes, while fasting, he ate no more than six grains of rice a day. Siddhartha grew very thin, but he was no closer to finding **enlightenment**. There just had to be another way. He was determined to find it.

One day, Siddhartha was wandering along the Nairanjana River when he came across a large fig tree that Siddhartha's followers would later call the

> *Siddhartha grew very thin, but he was no closer to finding enlightenment.*

People and Terms to Know

Ganges (GAN·JEEZ) **River**—river of north India and present-day Bangladesh. It rises in the Himalaya Mountains and flows 1,560 miles eastward to the Bay of Bengal.

enlightenment—wisdom. In Buddhism, this is a final blessed state marked by the absence of desire or suffering.

bodhi tree. He sat down on the grass beneath the tree. There Siddhartha vowed that he would not move until he had discovered how to end suffering.

There was a way a person could escape the cycle of rebirth and suffering.

He sat there day after day. He thought about the pain and suffering of human beings. He thought about the endless cycle of birth, death, and rebirth. Then it occurred to him that people could influence their rebirth by their behavior in this life. Good deeds would lead to a good life upon **reincarnation**. Evil deeds would lead to another lifetime of misery.

Siddhartha had been sitting and thinking for forty-nine days. Then it came to him. There was a way a person could escape the cycle of rebirth and suffering. A person could separate himself or herself from the things that caused suffering—all of life's pleasures, including family, possessions, and comforts. Then a person could reach **nirvana**, or perfect peace. There would no longer be a need to

---

People and Terms to Know

bodhi (BOH•dee) **tree**—"enlightenment tree," name given to the fig tree under which the Buddha gained enlightenment.

reincarnation—rebirth in a new body or in a new form of life.

nirvana (neer•VAH•nuh)—final state of bliss that overcomes all suffering, sought by Buddhists.

be reborn to suffer again. At this instant, Siddhartha had become the Buddha, the Enlightened One.

Siddhartha decided that the time had come to go forth into the world as the Buddha. It was time to help bring an end to the suffering of others. He walked to Sarnath, four miles north of the city of **Benares**. There, in the Deer Park, he found five companions who had been with him earlier in his wanderings. Here the Buddha gave his first sermon. These five companions became his first disciples.

The Buddha's teachings consisted of Four Noble Truths and an Eightfold Path, by which anyone could attain nirvana. Before long, the *dharma*—Buddha's teachings—had spread far and wide, as Buddha and his followers journeyed from place to place.

One day Buddha arrived back in Kapilavastu. King Suddhodhana realized that his son had achieved enlightenment. The king bowed down before him and asked to be accepted as a disciple. Buddha's wife Yasodhara and his son Rahula left the palace to follow him. After many more years of travel, Buddha died at the age of eighty. He was at peace with himself and the world, having preached for forty-five years.

People and Terms to Know

Benares (buh•NAHR•uhs)—ancient city on the Ganges River in northern India. (See the map on page 18.)

Buddha's Teachings

In his Sermon at Sarnath, Buddha taught that anyone who follows the Four Noble Truths and the Eightfold Path can attain enlightenment and reach nirvana, a final state of bliss and freedom from suffering.

The Four Noble Truths

First Noble Truth Everything in life is suffering and sorrow.

Second Noble Truth The cause of all suffering is people's selfish desire for the temporary pleasures of this world.

Third Noble Truth The way to end all suffering is to end all desires.

Fourth Noble Truth The way to overcome such desires and attain enlightenment is to follow the Eightfold Path. This is the Middle Way between desires and self-denial.

The Eightfold Path

Right Views

Right Resolve

Right Speech

Right Conduct

Right Livelihood

Right Effort

Right Mindfulness

Right Concentration

QUESTIONS TO CONSIDER

1. Why was King Suddhodhana worried about his son Siddhartha's future?

2. What did King Suddhodhana do to prevent Siddhartha from going out into the world?

3. Why did Siddhartha leave everything and everyone dear to him?

4. According to the Buddha, what causes suffering in the world?

Buddha
by Demi

Author-illustrator Demi, a Buddhist herself, retells the story of Siddhartha, the prince of ancient India who abandons his life of luxury to seek the answer to the problem of human suffering.

I Was Once a Monkey: Stories Buddha Told
by Jeanne M. Lee

Jeanne M. Lee retells a group of the Buddhist fables known as Jataka tales. These tales were originally told by the Buddha to his followers to illustrate how they should treat others. The Jataka tales feature animal characters, which are often the Buddha himself in one of his previous lives.

Buddhism
by Catherine Hewitt

Catherine Hewitt presents the history of Buddhism and describes its beliefs and practices.

Confucius Says...

BY STEPHEN CURRIE

Early that morning the gossip began. It flew around the court from one person to the next, like a little bird with a wagging tongue. The **duke of Lu** was ill, whispered a kitchen maid. No, the royal breakfast had been burned, said a carpenter. No, bad news had been received from abroad, insisted a tax collector. As always, there were a hundred different people, telling a hundred different stories. I readied my brush and my ink and my scrolls. As the duke's official scribe, I knew I would soon enough hear the truth.

Indeed, well before the midday meal, the duke called me. I am ashamed to say I took my time. It was a clear, crisp spring morning, and I took a

---

People and Terms to Know

duke of Lu (loo)—ruler of a province in China during the sixth century B.C. At one point, the duke hired Confucius to serve in the government.

This portrait of Confucius was made by rubbing on paper placed over an inked stone carving.

roundabout route through the royal gardens on my way to his side. There were a good many roses in full bloom, and even more birds flitting about singing. Their charms are always hard to resist. So I was a few minutes late arriving at the court.

The duke wore his finest robes and sat on his official seat. His face was red and his eyes bulged with fury. It was clear that he was having great difficulty controlling himself. At first, I stayed back, fearing that I had angered him by being late. But I quickly saw that this was not the case. Instead, he was glaring at three men who stood across from him. I knew them all—the duke's librarian, the head gardener, and the chief cook. Their hands were tied by ropes, and an armed guard stood behind each one. The men looked frightened, worried, and, most of all, miserable. Indeed, I had never before seen three such miserable men.

I made a bow, gave an apology, and began to set up my tools. Only then did I happen to notice the other man in the room. My head jerked up, and I drew a deep breath. "**Confucius**," I whispered.

People and Terms to Know

Confucius (kuhn•FYOO•shuhs)—Chinese philosopher, teacher, and minor government official who lived from 551 to 479 B.C. Today, millions of people follow his ideas.

Confucius! I had often heard of this great man, a philosopher and thinker who lived here in Lu. He sometimes advised the duke on important matters.

Confucius was trying to tame society—to bring back goodness and respect.

The problem with China, Confucius often said, was that it was not moral enough. These were troubled times. People cheated one another and were quick to use violence. Even those who seemed honest too often turned out to be the opposite. Confucius was trying to tame society—to bring back goodness and respect. And, even if you preferred the teachings of his rival, <u>Laozi</u>, you had to see that much of what Confucius said was true.

I could not believe my great good luck. I had seen his portrait, of course, but I had never seen Confucius in person. I bowed low, so low my brushes tumbled from my grasp. Embarrassed, I picked them up and bowed a second time. The great man gravely returned my bow, which impressed me. After all, I was only a simple scribe

People and Terms to Know

Laozi (LOW•DZUH)—founder of Daoism (DOW•IHZ•uhm), a Chinese moral philosophy with many followers in China and elsewhere today. Daoism stresses people's relationship to the *Dao* ("Way"), a universal force in nature. It is believed that Laozi was a historian in a royal palace during the sixth century B.C.

and he was—well, he was Confucius. I bowed a third time, just to be sure.

"The modest are near to virtue," Confucius told me. "But two bows would have been sufficient," he added.

He had spoken directly to me! This time I was so excited, I managed to drop my scroll.

"I will come right to the point." The duke scowled at the three men opposite him. "One of these three is a thief. One of these men has stolen a precious **jade** piece from my collection, a small green bird about the size of my hand."

I wrote furiously, trying to keep up with the flow of words. The story was clear enough. The piece was extremely valuable. Why, the jade alone was worth thousands. The carving was beautiful. It was among the duke's favorite pieces of art. It had occupied a place of honor in the palace.

"Last night, it was in my chambers," the duke concluded. "This morning, it was gone. My guards saw these men and no others near my chambers during the night. Therefore, one of them must have taken it." He turned to Confucius. "Is it not so?"

People and Terms to Know

jade—gemstone that is usually green or white in color. The Chinese considered jade the most precious of all gems.

"The cautious seldom make mistakes," the great man said.

I unrolled one more scroll and wrote down Confucius's words. It was easy to see what he was getting at. Instead of accusing everybody in sight, Confucius was saying, wait and hear the evidence.

"Oh," murmured the duke. "I see . . ." He frowned. "Well, what have you got to say for yourselves?"

"My lord," said the librarian, "I am a simple man, and I have simple tastes. I was at your chambers to bring you a book of poetry. I came with the book, and I left with nothing." He licked his lip nervously and went on. "I do not have this bird. I have never seen it. You may search my chambers, my library, my person. I have worked for you these ten years and more. Surely you cannot think, you must not think, that I would ever—"

"The cautious seldom make mistakes," the great man said.

Confucius tapped his chin. "To go beyond is as wrong as to fall short," he said gently.

I smiled to myself. Again, the great man's meaning was clear. The librarian was protesting too much. I dipped my brush into the ink and wrote.

An ancient jade bird from the Shang period (c. 1532–1027 B.C.).

The gardener spoke up. "I have also never seen the piece, my lord. I know nothing of this small green bird in flight. I came to your chambers to tell you that your roses were in bloom, but you did not speak with me. When I tried to tell you again this morning, I was seized. I was not told why until just now." His eyes brimmed with tears. "The roses are beautiful, my lord. I have worked *hard*, my lord—"

The great man cleared his throat. All eyes turned to him. "Things that are done, it is needless to speak about," he said.

I nodded and wrote. Confucius was quite right. The beauty of the roses had nothing to do with the missing piece.

"I—" The cook seemed tongue-tied. "I—only wanted to ask you about the menu, my lord, that was all. I—" His voice trailed off. "I didn't know about any jade bird . . ."

"When you do not know a thing, to admit that you do not know it," said Confucius, "that is wisdom."

> *"Maybe I should just choose one and put him in jail," sighed the duke. "A little torture—"*

"Maybe I should just choose one and put him in jail," sighed the duke. "A little torture—"

The librarian gasped. The gardener turned pale. The cook's eyes bulged with fear.

"The best kind of man," said Confucius, "does not set his mind either for or against anything. What is right is what he will follow."

The duke sighed. "I asked you here to help me, not to recite riddles with no point."

Confucius stirred and leaned forward. "I am not one who was born in the possession of knowledge."

I wrote quickly. To me, Confucius's meaning was clear. Knowledge was gained by listening, not by thinking that you knew all the answers already. Careful listening could tell us the truth—could tell us which man had stolen the piece. I stretched the scroll and looked back at what I had written—

Suddenly I knew where the jade piece was, and who had taken it.

I put down my brush. "My lord?" My voice was husky and low. "My lord, if I may . . ."

"Yes, scribe?" The duke frowned in my direction.

I got to my feet and bowed; then bowed again. "My lord, if you would send a guard into the royal garden, you will find your jade bird," I said. It was on the branch of a bush, I explained. I told him as nearly as I could exactly which one and where.

"What?" The cry came from the gardener. "My lord, you must not—"

The duke silenced him with a look. He nodded to one of the guards, who left the room. A minute or two later he returned with a small green bird. Its wings were outstretched as if in flight.

"Very impressive!" said the duke. "And a good place to hide a bird—in a garden with dozens of others just like it. Tell me, scribe, how did you know?"

"I was in the garden this morning," I said, not explaining how I had come to be there. "I saw a great many birds. All were singing, except one, *this* one. I thought perhaps it was mute. But as I listened to you and these men, I realized that it was your piece of art."

Confucius smiled. "Virtue is at hand," he murmured. My chest swelled with pride.

The gardener's lip curled. "That means nothing," he argued. "Other people use the garden. Someone else may have stolen the bird and hidden it. You have no proof—"

"Oh, but I do," I said, and slowly I unrolled the scroll before me. "All three of you said you had never seen it. My lord the duke described it to us." I found the exact words and read them back. "He called it 'a small green bird about the size of my hand.'"

"And?" demanded the gardener.

I took the figure from the guard and set it in my palm, being especially careful of the outstretched wings. "The duke said nothing about the position of the bird. But you alone knew that the figure showed a bird in flight." I jabbed my forefinger at his words from earlier that morning. "In flight."

"How did you know that," I asked him, "if you had never seen the bird before?"

The gardener's body sagged, and the life went out of his eyes.

"Put him in the dungeon," sighed the duke.

"The best kind of man is modest in his speech," said Confucius, "but does well in his actions." And he smiled broadly at me.

QUESTIONS TO CONSIDER

1. Why do you think that Confucius used short, riddlelike statements to explain his philosophy instead of telling people directly what he meant?

2. What did Confucius mean when he said, "Things that are done, it is needless to speak about"?

3. Which of the quotations from Confucius seems to you to still apply today? Why?

The Sayings of Confucius

The followers of Confucius made a collection of his sayings soon after his death. Here are a few examples.

"He who rules by means of his virtue may be compared to the North Star, which keeps its place and all the stars turn towards it."

"Learn as if you were chasing something you could not quite reach, and were always afraid of losing."

"Learning without thought is wasted effort; thought without learning is dangerous."

"Chi Wan thought three times before he acted. When the Master was told of this, he said, 'Twice is enough.'"

"With only rice to eat, water to drink, and my bended arm for a pillow—I have still joy in the midst of these things. Riches and honors gained by wickedness, are to me as a floating cloud."

Fa Mulan: The Story of a Woman Warrior
by Robert D. San Souci

Confucius believed that children should sacrifice themselves for their parents. Robert D. San Souci retells the famous Chinese legend of the brave girl who disguises herself as a boy and takes her father's place in the Khan's army to fight invaders.

Confucianism
by Thomas and Dorothy Hoobler

The Hooblers describe how the teachings of Confucius developed from a philosophy to a religion, and how Confucianism has shaped Chinese culture for over 2,000 years.

Taoism
by Paula R. Hartz

The Chinese philosophy of Taoism was founded by Laozi, who lived around the same time as Confucius. Paula R. Hertz presents an introduction to Taoism, which has been Confucianism's greatest rival in influencing Chinese culture.

Shi Huangdi, the First Emperor

BY WALTER HAZEN

My name is Sung Po. I am a <u>scholar</u> who is very lucky to be alive. Liu Yu and Ko Heng, my dear friends, were not so lucky. Liu was killed by order of **Shi Huangdi**. Ko died working on the **Great Wall**.

Wait. Forgive me. I am far ahead of my story. At this point, I should tell you who Shi Huangdi is. Or maybe I should say "was," for he has been dead some ten years now. And the Great Wall? You may

---

People and Terms to Know

scholar—learned person; one who studies and makes knowledge his or her life's work.

Shi Huangdi (shihr•hwahng•dee)—first emperor of a unified China. He ruled from 221 to 207 B.C. He also is remembered for building China's Great Wall.

Great Wall—border wall in northern China built to keep out invaders.

Hundreds of life-size clay warriors were found in the tomb of Emperor Shi Huangdi at the ancient Chinese capital of Xian.

have heard of it, but do you know how it came to be? I will tell you this and more.

I was living in the city of Xianyang (shyen•yahng) when Shi Huangdi became China's first emperor. His real name was Cheng. He had been the ruler of the western state of **Ch'in**. When he was crowned emperor, he took the title "Huangdi."

"Our ruler is more than a king. He is a mighty emperor."

When this happened, my young son Wen asked me a question. "Father, why does the emperor take the title 'Huangdi'? Doesn't 'Wang' mean 'king'?"

"Ah, son," I replied. "Our ruler is more than a king. He is a mighty emperor. He has conquered and unified all of China. That is why he has chosen to be called 'Huangdi.' Huangdi means 'emperor.'"

About twenty years before becoming emperor of China, Shi Huangdi was crowned king of Ch'in. He was twelve at the time. People say he forced his father to kill himself and that he treated his mother terribly. I cannot say with any

People and Terms to Know

Ch'in (chihn)—one of the states, or divisions, of early China.

▲

The Great Wall protected 1,500 miles of ancient China's northern border.

certainty that these things happened. Szuma Ch'ien, the historian, swears these things are true.

As the king of Ch'in, Shi Huangdi chose a man named Li Ssu as his chief advisor. It was a wise move. Li Ssu was a capable official who guided Shi in his early years. With Li Ssu's help, Shi brought the other Chinese states under his control and set himself up as emperor. Then Li Ssu became his **prime minister**.

People and Terms to Know

prime minister—chief government official.

My son Wen is now thirty, but he never tires of quizzing me about the small role I played in the short rule of Shi Huangdi.

As I told Wen, about seven years after Shi Huangdi became emperor, he made a decision that cost the lives of many of my friends. He didn't come up with the idea himself. The idea to burn all the books came from Li Ssu.

"Father," Wen would ask, "why would the emperor order the thoughts of Confucius and others to be destroyed?"

"Well," I replied, "Confucius believed that rulers should set a good example for their people. If the ruler was wise and behaved well, his people would behave well also. Li Ssu didn't agree."

Shi Huangdi ordered all scholars to turn in all books about Confucius and his teachings.

Li Ssu believed in a clear set of laws that were to be strictly enforced. He wanted nothing to do with Confucius and his kind. So Shi Huangdi ordered all scholars to turn in all books about Confucius and his teachings. These and all histories except those of Ch'in were to be burned. Only books about science were kept.

Many scholars obeyed the emperor's order. They gathered together copies of the books and brought them in. Other scholars did not. My friends Liu Yu and Ko Heng were among those who did not give up their books. Both lost their lives because they refused. Liu Hu did not suffer, for he was beheaded quickly. Ko Heng worked for two years at the Great Wall and died of exhaustion and overwork.

I was among the few who found a way out. True, I obeyed the emperor's order and turned in my books. But before I did, I memorized Confucius's most important works and sayings. That way I was able to help keep his great thoughts alive and pass them on to others. Shortly after Shi Huangdi died, books containing Confucius's teachings began to reappear.

In addition to burning priceless books, Shi Huangdi wiped out many of China's most powerful families. He seized the land of 120,000 noble families and forced them to move to the capital where he could keep an eye on them. He called this "strengthening the trunk and weakening the branches." Anyone who plotted against him was immediately killed.

By now you might be thinking that Shi Huangdi was a harsh ruler who treated his people terribly. He was. But he also did great things during his fourteen-year rule. Not the least of his achievements was the Great Wall. Many of my friends, along with thousands of poor farmers, died working on it. But it is a sight to behold.

After ten years, the Great Wall was completed.

QUESTIONS TO CONSIDER

1. What methods did Shi Huangdi use to control his subjects and keep power?

2. Why did Shi Huangdi order the works of Confucius burned?

3. How did the changes made by Shi Huangdi help to unify China?

4. What do you think the expression "strengthening the trunk and weakening the branches" means?

5. How do you think Confucius would have judged Shi Huangdi as a ruler?

The Great Wall of China

China's Great Wall is about 1,500 miles long. It twists and turns like a dragon's tail along China's northern border, from the Yellow Sea in the east to the Gobi Desert in the west.

The Great Wall is 25 feet high, with 40-foot watchtowers every 200 to 300 yards. Its base is 25 feet thick. The outside of the wall is covered with stone slabs. The inner core holds stone, dirt, and rubble.

When Shi Huangdi came to power, sections of the wall already existed. They had been built to keep northern invaders out. Shi Huangdi decided to join these sections together and to extend the wall thousands of miles. He forced hundreds of thousands of peasants to labor for ten years to build it. Many who died working on the wall were buried inside it.

Work continued on the Great Wall under later Chinese rulers. It kept out invaders until the thirteenth century, when the Mongol leader Genghis Khan broke through and conquered northern China.

The Tomb of Princess Tou Wan

BY MARIANNE McCOMB

The day was hot and dusty. The heat was terrible, and it wasn't even noon yet. But the dust—that was the worst. It was everywhere, and there was no hiding from it. Kwong pulled his kerchief over his nose and tugged at his hard hat on his head. "This is a tough way to make a living," he thought to himself grimly. "We've been here for months now, and still we're not ready to begin construction of the new hospital."

Kwong was the foreman of a work crew. He had been hired by the Chinese government to build a new hospital in the northeastern part of China. (See the map on page 21.) The year was 1955, and Kwong was lucky to have the work.

Kwong's boss rushed toward him. "Kwong, I'd like that dirt pile over there cleared before lunch."

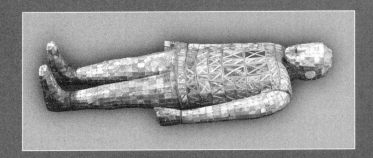

Princess Tou Wan's burial suit was made from more than 2,000 plates of jade held together with gold wire. The ancient Chinese believed that jade could preserve a body. The inset shows the entire burial suit.

Kwong looked over at the dirt pile. It was more than 20 feet high! He would need to put his whole crew on the job. Still, he knew what to say. "I'll have my men over there immediately, sir. And thank you for the opportunity." Kwong bowed and hurried off.

Soon Kwong and his men were hard at work. Two workers sat behind the wheel of a huge bulldozer. The rest manned the shovels. Kwong urged the men to dig faster.

Suddenly, Kwong heard a loud clang. The diggers had hit something with their shovels.

Suddenly, Kwong heard a loud clang. The diggers had hit something with their shovels. The men cleared away a thin layer of dirt and found some large stones. The stones were flat and had been carefully shaped at the edges. On the face of each stone was some ancient Chinese writing.

Kwong and his men lifted the strange stones out of the dirt pile. Underneath they found a rock slab that was as large as fifteen men. This too was covered in ancient writing. With growing excitement, Kwong realized that he and his men had found something important. He looked over at his work crew and said excitedly, "Hold up, men! I think we've got something here!"

*   *   *

Although he didn't know it at the time, Kwong and his crew had found more than just *something*. In fact, they had made one of the most amazing **archaeological** discoveries of all time. The 20-foot dirt pile that stood in the way of the new hospital was really an ancient burial mound that had been untouched for centuries.

The Chinese government knew that the burial mound was important. Government officials called in archaeologists to supervise the dig. All thoughts of the new hospital were forgotten as the archaeological team carefully lifted the rock slab out of the mound. Kwong, who was allowed to observe the dig, watched as the archaeologists sifted through bucket loads of dirt.

Four months later, the team had cleared a 52-foot pit. At the bottom of the pit were thick layers of earth, white clay, and charcoal. Kwong helped the archaeologists chip away at the layers. At last, the workers struck something solid with their tools.

"This is it!" one of the archaeologists called out. "We've found a door of some type!" The workers carefully pried open the door. Kwong peered inside.

People and Terms to Know

archaeological (AHR•kee•uh•LAHJ•ih•kuhl)—relating to the study of ancient civilizations.

"My my!" he breathed. "What have we found?"

*   *   *

Inside the door was a tomb filled with the most amazing treasures Kwong had ever seen. There were colorful silks, beautiful sculptures, delicate **porcelain**, and shimmering jewels beyond belief!

"It's not so unusual to find riches in a burial tomb," one of the archaeologists explained to Kwong. "The ancient Chinese believed in life after death. They buried food, personal belongings, and even animals with their dead. They were sure these items would come in handy in the afterlife. It looks to me like some of these riches may date back to the **Han dynasty**."

"How do you know?" Kwong asked with interest.

"I see a couple of important clues," the archaeologist answered. "First, you may remember from your history books that the Han period was one of relative peace in China. Wars were few and far

---

People and Terms to Know

porcelain (PAWR•suh•lihn)—like china, a hard, white material made by baking fine clay. The Chinese are known for their beautiful porcelain.

Han dynasty—period of an ancient ruling family. The Hans ruled China from 206 B.C. to A.D. 220. They put a centralized government in place and brought peace and stability to China.

between. So, people could develop practical and beautiful things. Many turned to arts and crafts. The Han period is known for its incredible artwork. Artists used silk, bronze, iron, and **lacquer**. They made beautiful tapestries, sculptures, and pottery.

"Notice also the fancy markings decorating the walls of the tomb. People of the Han period—especially royalty—would pay a small fortune to make sure a funeral was perfect. Those who wanted to gain great respect from others would spend months or even years looking for just the right burial spot. Once they found a good place, they'd order the finest coffin money could buy. Then artists were hired to create very detailed paintings or carvings for the walls of the tomb. Royal men and women insisted on having beautiful scenes painted or carved inside their tombs."

"Do you think this tomb was built for a royal person?" Kwong asked excitedly.

"It's possible," the archaeologist answered. "You can tell that this tomb held the body of someone important because the carvings on the wall are so detailed. It would have taken many artists many months to create such magnificent murals."

People and Terms to Know

lacquer (LAK•uhr)—glossy coating given to objects of wood, clay or metal.

While Kwong and the archaeologist were talking, another group was digging through the riches. They found a wooden box that was obviously a coffin. Inside the coffin was another coffin. Inside that one was still another. Altogether there were six coffins.

Kwong and the archaeologists looked inside. At first they could not believe their eyes.

The researchers carefully pried off the lid of the innermost coffin. Kwong and the archaeologists looked inside. At first they could not believe their eyes.

Resting inside the innermost coffin was the body of a woman that was almost perfectly preserved. She wore an elaborate jade suit that covered her body from chin to toe. Over the top part of her face was a mask made of small pieces of jade, bits of gold, and small jewels.

Kwong and the others were amazed. This woman, who had been dead for centuries, looked as if she were sleeping peacefully. Surely this was one of the most incredible archaeological finds of all time!

*   *   *

Many months later, Kwong read a newspaper story about the woman in the jade suit. Archaeologists discovered that her name was

Princess Tou Wan. She did in fact live during the Han dynasty. Princess Tou Wan was the wife of Prince Liu Sheng, who was the son of the Han dynasty's Emperor Ching. The clay, charcoal, and wood inside her tomb had made it completely airtight. That was why her body had not decayed over the centuries.

Researchers could tell a lot about Princess Tou Wan. She was around fifty years old when a heart attack killed her. The princess was overweight. She once had broken her arm. An autopsy revealed a few melon seeds in her stomach. She must have eaten melon shortly before she died. Kwong and the archaeologists had been right. Princess Tou Wan in her coffin was an amazing archaeological discovery.

QUESTIONS TO CONSIDER

1. How would you have felt if you had been with Kwong and the archaeologist when they discovered the tomb of Princess Tou Wan?

2. Before the tomb was opened, why did the archaeologist believe someone important was buried inside?

3. In what ways do the burial customs of the ancient Chinese differ from burial customs in the United States today?

4. What do you think about scientists digging up Princess Tou Wan?

Sources

Imhotep and the First Pyramid *by Lynnette Brent*
Miralai and Dalaja are fictional characters. Imhotep and the pharaoh Djoser are historical figures. There are many sources of information about life in ancient Egypt and the building of the Step Pyramid. One is *The Egyptians: An Introduction to Egyptian Archaeology* by John Ruffle (Ithaca, NY: Cornell University Press, 1977). Another is *When Egypt Ruled the East* by George Steindorff and Keith C. Seele (Chicago, IL: The University of Chicago Press).

His Majesty, Herself: Hatshepsut of Egypt *by Dee Masters*
Ineni, Amenhotep, Hatshepsut, and Thutmose are historical figures. The story is based on the writings in Ineni's tomb, which he himself built. Sources include *Hatshepsut: The Female Pharaoh* by Joyce Tyldesley (Penguin USA, 1998).

Akhenaten and Nefertiti *by Judith Lloyd Yero*
All major characters are real. The scenes describe events that are typical of daily life during Akhenaten's reign. A good source for information about Akhenaten is *Akhenaten and the Religion of Light* by Erik Hornung, translated by David Lorton (Ithaca, NY: Cornell University Press, 1999).

An Ethiopian Tale: The Queen of Sheba *by Stephen Currie*
The daughter and her letters are fiction. The earliest information about Solomon and Sheba is found in Jewish religious writings and also appears in the Book of Esther in the Old Testament of the Bible and in the Qur'an. The classical Ethiopian history, written in the 14th century is called *Kebra Negast,* or Glory of the Kings. It includes the story of Solomon and Sheba.

King Sargon and the Curse of Agade *by Marianne McComb*

The story's narrator is fictional. The information about Sargon and his Akkadian empire is factually accurate. The legend of the goddess Ishtar is from ancient Mesopotamian tradition. A good source of information about this ancient civilization is *Ancient Iraq* by Georges Roux (Cleveland, OH: World Publishing Company, 1965).

The Story of Gilgamesh *by Walter Hazen*

The characters in this story are legendary, although scholars believe that Gilgamesh was an early king of Uruk. The epic is known to us today because an Assyrian king who lived in the seventh century B.C. had the ancient story translated into Akkadian and inscribed in cuneiform characters on twelve clay tablets. The original story was probably told in the Babylonian language about 2000 B.C. *The Epic of Gilgamesh* translated by N. D. Sandars is available in the Penguin Classics series (Penguin Books, Ltd., 1964). Secondary sources about the epic include *Gods, Graves, and Scholars* by C. W. Ceram (New York: Alfred A. Knopf, 1961) and *Cradle of Civilization* by Samuel Noah Kramer and the editors of Time-Life Books (New York: Time, Inc., 1967).

Tale of a Tablet House *by Stephen Feinstein*

Akki and his parents Gamil and Puabi are fictional. The information presented in the story is factually accurate. We know a great deal about the activities of scribes and about Sumerian life from the fragments of tablets that have been found and translated by scholars. One source is *The Quest for Sumer* by Leonard Cottrell (New York: G. P. Putnam's Sons, 1965). Information about women's lives can be found in *Women's Roles in Ancient Mesopotamia: A Reference Guide* by Bella Vivante (Westport, CT: Greenwood Press, 1999).

Hammurabi's Code *by Lynnette Brent*

Adad, Siduri, Hanish, and Shullat are fictional characters and their story is fiction. The details about the way of life described in the story and the information about the code are factually accurate. You can learn more in *Babylonians* by H.W.F. Saggs (Norman: University of Oklahoma Press, 1995).

The Story of Ruth *from the Bible as retold by Fitzgerald Higgins*

Naomi, Ruth, Orpah, and Boaz are found in the Book of Ruth in the Old Testament of the Bible. Information about Israelite civilization in the 11th century B.C. is based on Jewish tradition. Sources include *Reconstructing the Society of Ancient Israel* by Paula McNutt (Louisville, KY: Westminster John Knox Press, London SPCK, 1999) and *Oxford History of the Biblical World* edited by Michael D. Coogan (New York: Oxford University Press, 1998).

Mohenjo-Daro: A Mystery *by Dee Masters*

Huan and Dr. Dani are fictional characters. Information about this ancient Indus Valley civilization is based on the work of archaeologists who have uncovered the city. Jonathan Mark Kenoyer describes the cities and gives his conclusions in his illustrated book *Ancient Cities of the Indus Valley Civilization* (New York: Oxford University Press, 1998). Another source is "Indus: Clues to an Ancient Civilization" in *National Geographic,* vol. 197, no. 6, June 2000.

Life of the Buddha *by Stephen Feinstein*

Siddhartha Gautama, his father King Suddhodhana, his mother Queen Mahamaya, his wife Yasodhara, his charioteer Chandaka, and his son Rahula all figure in the *Pali Tipitaka,* which is the earliest book of the Buddha's teachings. It was put together by Buddhist monks in the years immediately after his death. There are many modern versions of his life and teachings in libraries. Story sources include *Prince Siddhartha: The Story of Buddha* by Jonathan Landaw (Boston: Wisdom Publications, 1984) and *Buddha* by Joan Lebold Cohen (New York: A Seymour Lawrence Book, Delacorte Press, 1969).

Confucius Says . . . *by Stephen Currie*

This little mystery story, its narrator, and the three suspects are all modern fiction. The duke of Lu and Confucius are historical figures. The teachings of Confucius were collected and written down by his followers about one generation after his death. They are preserved in a book known in the West as the *Analects*. In them, Confucius's teachings are described as if they were part of a conversation. Here also Confucius describes himself and his own discovery of wisdom. A modern source is *Confucius* by Raymond Stanley Dawson (New York: Hill and Wang, 1982).

Shi Huangdi, the First Emperor *by Walter Hazen*

Sung Po, his son Wen, and his friends Liu Yu and Ko Heng are fictional characters. The emperor Shi Huangdi and his prime minister Li Ssu are historical figures, and the events described here are historically accurate. Sources of information include *Our Oriental Heritage,* volume 1 in historian Will Durant's Story of Civilization series (New York: Simon and Schuster, 1935) and *Ancient China* by Edward H. Schaefer and the editors of Time-Life Books (New York: Time, Inc., 1967).

The Tomb of Princess Tou Wan *by Marianne McComb*

Kwong is a fictional character, but the archaeological dig that discovered Princess Tou Wan's tomb is real. China's first major historian, Qian Sima, lived during the Han dynasty. His history can now be read in an English translation, *Records of the Grand Historian* (New York: Columbia University Press, 1993). A source of information about life during the Han dynasty is *Divination, Mythology and Monarchy in Han China* by Michael Loewe (Cambridge: University of Cambridge Oriental Publications, No. 48, 1995). The source for the discovery of Princess Tou Wan's tomb is *Secrets from the Past* by Gene S. Stuart (Washington, DC: National Geographic Society, 1979)

Glossary of People and Terms to Know

Akhenaten (AH•kuhn•NAHT•n)
—Egyptian pharaoh who reigned
from 1353 to 1336 B.C.

Akhetaten (AH•keh•TAH•tehn)—
city built by Akhenaten to honor
the god of the sun. Today, the site
of Akhetaten is called Tel el-Amarna.
The reign of Akhenaten is often
called the "Period of Amarna."

Akkad (AK•ad)—ancient country
in what is now Iraq.

Amenhotep I
(AH•muhn•HOH•tehp)—
Hatshepsut's grandfather, a
pharaoh who ruled from about
1514 to 1493 B.C. He invaded
Nubia and fought wars with the
Libyans and Syrians.

Amenhotep III
(AH•muhn•HOH•tehp)—Egyptian
pharaoh who ruled from 1390 to
1353 B.C. He built many statues
and temples, especially at Karnak.
He broke tradition by marrying
Tiye, a commoner from the African
kingdom of Nubia.

archaeological
(AHR•kee•uh•LAHJ•ih•kuhl)—
relating to the study of ancient
civilizations.

archaeologist
(AHR•kee•AHL•uh•jist)—
scientist who studies ancient
civilizations.

artifacts—objects remaining
from early civilizations. Even
broken pieces of artifacts
interest archaeologists.

Aten (AHT•n)—Egyptian
god representing the power
behind the sun god, Re. Aten is
shown as a circle representing the
golden disk of the sun.

Babylon (BAB•uh•luhn)—capital
of the ancient Babylonian Empire.
It was located on the Euphrates
River in southwest Asia.

Benares (buh•NAHR•uhs)—
ancient city on the Ganges River
in northern India.

Bethlehem—ancient town in
Israel on the west bank of the
Jordan River south of Jerusalem.

**black land and the red land,
the**—rich, black farmland around
the Nile River and the red
desert sands.

bodhi (BOH•dee) **tree**—
"enlightenment tree," name given
to the fig tree under which the
Buddha gained enlightenment.

Brahmans (BRAH•muhnz)—
Hindu priests who served the creator god Brahma.

Ch'in (chihn)—one of the states,
or divisions, of early China.

city-states—self-governing states,
each made up of a single major
city and the surrounding area.

Confucius (kuhn•FYOO•shuhs)—
Chinese philosopher, teacher, and
minor government official who
lived from 551 to 479 B.C. Today,
millions of people follow his ideas.

cremate—reduce a dead body to
ashes by burning.

cuneiform
(KYOO•nee•uh•FAWRM)—ancient
Mesopotamian form of writing.
Cuneiform was the world's first
form of writing. It was invented by
Sumerian scribes around 3000 B.C.

David—(died c. 962) second king
of Israel and traditional author of
many of the Psalms in the Bible.

Djoser (ZHOH•suhr)—Egyptian pharaoh who ruled from about 2650 to 2575 B.C. He is best known for building the pyramid at Saqqara.

duke of Lu (loo)—ruler of a province in China during the sixth century B.C. At one point, the duke hired Confucius to serve in the government.

enlightenment—wisdom. In Buddhism, this is a final blessed state marked by the absence of desire or suffering.

epic—long poem or tale about the adventurous deeds of gods and heroes.

Ethiopia (EE•thee•OH•pee•uh)—country in east central Africa.

Euphrates River (yoo•FRAY•teez)—river in southwest Asia. Today, it rises in Turkey, flows through Syria and Iraq, and eventually joins the Tigris River.

famine—severe, wide-reaching food shortage.

Ganges River (GAN•jeez)—river of north India and present-day Bangladesh. It rises in the Himalaya Mountains and flows 1,560 miles eastward to the Bay of Bengal.

Gilgamesh (GIHL•guh•MEHSH)—legendary Sumerian king who was the hero of Sumerian and Babylonian tales.

Great Wall—border wall in northern China built to keep out invaders.

Hammurabi (HAM•uh•RAH•bee)—king of the city-state of Babylon who ruled from about 1792 to 1750 B.C. Hammurabi conquered nearby city-states to create the Babylonian Empire, bringing all of Mesopotamia under one rule.

Hammurabi's Code—collection of 282 laws and edicts of the Babylonian Empire. Carved in stone, this code is the best-preserved legal document from an ancient civilization.

Han dynasty—period of an ancient ruling family. The Hans ruled China from 206 B.C. to A.D. 220. They put a centralized government in place and brought peace and stability to China.

Hatshepsut (hat•SHEP•soot)—first woman to be king (pharaoh) of Egypt. She ruled from about 1472 to 1458 B.C.

Imhotep (ihm•HOH•tehp)—poet, architect, and physician who served under four Egyptian pharaohs. He was chief architect for Djoser's pyramid at Saqqara. After his death, Egyptians made Imhotep a god.

Indus River Valley—wide valley made by the Indus River in present-day Pakistan. One of the world's earliest civilizations developed here.

Ineni (in•NEHN•nee)—Egyptian architect who built for several pharaohs.

Ishtar—in Sumerian legend, goddess of war, fertility, and love.

Israel (IHZ•ree•uhl)—ancient kingdom in southwest Asia on the eastern shore of the Mediterranean Sea.

jade—gemstone that is usually green or white in color. The Chinese considered jade the most precious of all gems.

judges—military rulers of ancient Israel between the time of Joshua and the establishment of the kingdom by Saul around 1020 B.C.

Karnak (KAHR•nak)—largest religious complex ever built. Karnak was built over thousands of years by many different pharaohs.

King Solomon—king of Israel during the tenth century B.C. Rich and the leader of a large and powerful empire, Solomon is probably best known for his wisdom. The phrase "wise as Solomon" is still common today.

kinsman—male relative; male member of the same extended family or clan.

lacquer (LAK•uhr)—glossy coating given to objects of wood, clay, or metal.

Laozi (LOW•DZUH)—founder of Daoism (DOW•IHZ•uhm), a Chinese moral philosophy with many followers in China and elsewhere today. Daoism stresses people's relationship to the *Dao* ("Way"), a universal force in nature. It is believed that Laozi was a historian in a royal palace during the sixth century B.C.

lapis lazuli (LAP•ihs LAZ•uh•lee)— dark blue, semiprecious stone used for jewelry.

Maat (muh•AHT)—Egyptian goddess of law and truth.

Moab (MOH•ab)—ancient kingdom east of the Dead Sea.

monotheism (MAHN•uh•THEE•iz•uhm)—belief in only one god or supreme being. Belief in multiple gods is called *polytheism*.

monsoon—wind system that brings very heavy summer rains to southern Asia.

Nefertiti (NEHF•uhr•TEE•tee)— queen of Egypt, considered a major advisor to Akhenaten, her husband. Her name means "the beautiful one has come."

nirvana (neer•VAH•nuh)—final state of bliss that overcomes all suffering, sought by Buddhists.

Noah—in the Bible, a man told by God to build an ark. This saved his family and one pair of each type of animal from a great flood that God caused to punish humans for being wicked.

papyrus (puh•PY•ruhs)—paper made from the pulp of the papyrus plant, a type of tall grass that grows in water.

pharaoh (FAIR•oh)—title of the kings of ancient Egypt.

porcelain (PAWR•suh•lihn)—like china, a hard, white material made by baking fine clay. The Chinese are known for their beautiful porcelain.

prime minister—chief government official.

Punt—ancient country in eastern Africa near present-day Somalia.

queen of Sheba—ruler of an ancient land that probably covered present-day Ethiopia in Africa and present-day Yemen in the Arabian Peninsula as well. She was known for her wisdom and wealth.

regent—temporary ruler until the real ruler can take over.

reincarnation—rebirth in a new body or in a new form of life.

Sargon (SAHR•gahn)— Mesopotamian military leader and king who ruled from about 2335 to 2279 B.C. Sargon was the first to unite all Mesopotamia under one ruler. His empire also reached beyond Mesopotamia.

scholar—learned person; one who studies and makes knowledge his or her life's work.

scribe—in ancient societies, one of the few people who could read and write. A scribe was an official who wrote the public records.

shard—broken piece of pottery.

Shi Huangdi (shihr hwahng•dee)— first emperor of a unified China. He ruled from 221 to 207 B.C. He also is remembered for building China's Great Wall.

Siddhartha Gautama (sid•DAHR•tuh GOW•tuh•muh)— (563–483 B.C.) the Buddha, Indian philosopher and founder of Buddhism. In the Sanskrit language, "Siddhartha" means "he who will accomplish." Today, over 340 million people in the world are Buddhist.

sphinxes (SFIHNGKS•ez)—figures in Egyptian mythology with the body of a lion and the head of a man, ram, or hawk.

step pyramid—high, step-shaped building that is both a tomb and a temple.

Sumer (SOO•muhr)—ancient region in the valley of the Euphrates River, north of its mouth.

terra cotta—baked clay pottery.

Thutmose I (thoot•MOH•suh)— Hatshepsut's father, pharaoh of Egypt from about 1493 to 1482 B.C. He is known for conquering Nubia in Africa and areas in Asia all the way to the Euphrates River.

turquoise—semiprecious blue-green stone used for jewelry.

Tutankhamen (TOOT•ahng•KAH•muhn)—Egyptian pharaoh who ruled from about 1333 to 1323 B.C., when he died at eighteen. This was the King Tut of history whose tomb, discovered in 1922, contained hundreds of treasures of ancient Egypt.

two Egypts—Upper and Lower Egypt. Upper Egypt was the southern region, up the Nile River. Lower Egypt was the northern region, downstream.

Ur—city of ancient Sumer located on the Euphrates River.

Valley of the Kings—place on the opposite bank of the Nile from Thebes. Hatshepsut's memorial temple and many royal tombs were built there.

zebu (ZEE•boo)—large Indian ox used for transportation and plowing.

Acknowledgements

8 © Hulton Getty Picture Library.
10 © Alinari/Art Resource.
12 © Associated Press AP.
13 © Tony Stone Images.
15, 17 © The Granger Collection.
22 © Glen Allison/Stone.
27 © The Granger Collection.
33 © Bettmann/Corbis.
36 © Francis G. Mayer/Corbis.
42 © Davis Factor/Corbis.
44 © ET Archive, London/
Superstock International.
46, 47 © The Granger Collection.
52 © ET Archive, London/
SuperStock International.
56 Francis G. Mayer/Corbis.
58, 65, 68 © Giraudon/Art
Resource, NY.
71 © Gianni Dagli Orti/Corbis.
79 © The Granger Collection.
83 © Bridgeman Art Library/
British Museum, London, UK.

89 © The Granger Collection.
93 © Gianni Dagli Orti/Corbis.
97 © The Granger Collection.
99 © The Pierpont Morgan
Library/Art Resource, NY.
102 © Richard T. Nowitz/Corbis.
108, 112 © Gianni Dagli Orti/Corbis.
117 © Borromeo/Art Resource, NY.
119 © Angelo Hornak/Corbis.
126 © Barney Burstein/Corbis.
138 © Corbis/Richard A. Cooke
140 © Hulton Getty Picture
Collection.
145 © The Granger Collection.
151 Glen Allison/Stone.
153 © Jerry Alexander/Stone.
155 © The Granger Collection.
161 © Asian Art & Archaeology/
Corbis.